U0617416

# 隐性分层教学法

## 在初中英语写作教学中的应用研究

李军强 著

黑龍江大學出版社
HEILONGJIANG UNIVERSITY PRESS
哈尔滨

**图书在版编目（CIP）数据**

隐性分层教学法在初中英语写作教学中的应用研究 / 李军强著 . -- 哈尔滨 : 黑龙江大学出版社 , 2024. 12.
ISBN 978-7-5686-1213-5

Ⅰ . G633.412

中国国家版本馆 CIP 数据核字第 2024RF8964 号

隐性分层教学法在初中英语写作教学中的应用研究
YINXING FENCENG JIAOXUEFA ZAI CHUZHONG YINGYU XIEZUO JIAOXUE ZHONG DE YINGYONG YANJIU
李军强　著

---

责任编辑　王瑞琦
出版发行　黑龙江大学出版社
地　　址　哈尔滨市南岗区学府三道街 36 号
印　　刷　亿联印刷（天津）有限公司
开　　本　720 毫米 ×1000 毫米　1/16
印　　张　13.25
字　　数　249 千
版　　次　2024 年 12 月第 1 版
印　　次　2024 年 12 月第 1 次印刷
书　　号　ISBN 978-7-5686-1213-5
定　　价　66.00 元

---

本书如有印装错误请与本社联系更换，联系电话：0451-86608666。

**版权所有　侵权必究**

# 序　言

在教学的道路上摸爬滚打的三十年中，我始终孜孜以求、不懈探索，看着学生们不断进步、有所收获，我心里总想着写点东西，以让自己的教育生涯不留遗憾。

在我的高中教学生涯中，我一直使用传统的英语写作教学法，也取得了一些教学成果。但是，自从我开始初中教学以来，我对初中学生书面表达与高中学生书面表达之间的差距倍感焦虑，于是，研究出更为适合的、更有效果的初中英语写作教学方法是我近年来的一大目标。在六年多的课堂教学实践中，我不断尝试、不断修正，在隐性分层写作教学的设计上费了许多心思、用了大量精力，终于总结出了基础层、提高层和发展层的隐性分层方法以及这一方法应用到初中英语写作教学中的具体途径。经过不断实验、不断修正、不断创新，我对这种教学法的应用逐渐熟练，帮助学生在英语写作方面取得很大进步。在初中学业水平考试等各类考试中，经历过这一教学法的学生的写作素养得到并经受住了检验。

本书共两章，第二章是本书核心，对义务教育教科书英语七年级、八年级、九年级（人民教育出版社 2013 年版）各单元写作教学具有一定的借鉴意义。希望本书的出版能为初中英语写作教学做出一点贡献。

作为一名教育工作者、一名一线教师，我将不忘初心、砥砺前行，不断提高自己、搞好教学，帮助更多学生取得成功与进步。

李军强

# 目　　录

# 第一章　理论综述

## 第一节　隐性分层教学法简介

隐性分层教学法是一种以学生为本,通过隐性分层手段实现个别化教育的教学方法。它充分考虑到学生现有水平的差异,通过分层施教、分层评价和个别辅导,使每个学生都能得到应有的进步。

初中英语写作教学的重要性不言而喻。写作是英语学习中一项重要的技能,它不仅涉及语言知识的运用,还涉及思维、表达和沟通能力。通过写作,学生可以更好地理解和掌握英语语言,提高英语综合能力。同时,写作教学也是初中英语教学中的重要组成部分,是体现英语教师教学水平的重要方面。然而,当前初中英语写作教学面临着一些共同挑战:

①学生词汇和语法知识的掌握程度不够。在写作过程中,学生需要用到大量的词汇和语法知识,但是很多学生由于词汇量不足、语法知识不扎实,写作中出现很多拼写和语法错误。

②写作教学方法单一。目前,很多教师在教授写作时,往往采用传统的"教师命题—学生写作—教师批改"这一教学模式,这种模式缺乏对学生写作过程的个性化指导和帮助,无法激发学生的学习兴趣和动力。

③学生写作技能的培养未得到足够重视。很多教师只注重对单词、语法等基础知识的讲解,而忽略了对学生写作技能的培养,导致学生在写作时无法准确地表达自己的想法。

④学生的阅读量小、语感弱。学生平时的英语阅读量较小,缺乏足够的语言输入,导致他们在写作时语感较弱,无法写出流畅、自然的文章。

为了应对这些挑战,教师需要不断探索新的教学方法和策略,注重培养学生的写作技能和语感,同时帮助学生提高对词汇和语法知识的运用能力。基于此,在初中英语写作教学中引入隐性分层教学法是非常必要的。使用这种教学方法,教师可以更好地关注每个学生的特点,促进他们在各自的基础上获得更好的发展。通过设置不同的教学目标、教学内容和教学方法,教师可以更好地满足不同层次学生的需求,有效激发他们的学习兴趣和动力,从而提高他们的英语写作水平。

## 一、理论背景

隐性分层教学法的理论基础包括因材施教理论、成功教育理论、合作学习理论以及掌握学习理论。

因材施教理论与隐性分层教学法的关系较为紧密。隐性分层教学法是在因材施教的原则下,针对不同层次的学生开展不同形式、不同内容的教学,使每个学生都能得到充分的发展。隐性分层是一种强调“隐性”的分类方法,因为教师通常不会公开学生所属的层次,以保护学生的自尊心。这种教学方法关注学生的个体差异,根据学生的知识水平、能力与倾向、兴趣与爱好等因素进行分类,为每个层次的学生制定个性化的教学方案。此外,因材施教理论强调教育要适应学生的个性特点,让每个学生的优势都得以发挥,促进学生的全面发展。隐性分层教学法正是因材施教理论在教学方法上的具体应用,它根据学生的实际情况,为每个学生提供适合其发展的教育资源和方法,使每个学生的潜能都能得到充分的挖掘和发挥。

成功教育理论与隐性分层教学法之间也存在一定联系。成功教育理论认为每个学生都有成功的可能,只是需要合适的机会和适当的引导。该理论强调教师的激励作用,认为教师应当关注学生的进步与成功,及时给予肯定和鼓励,以增强学生的自信心和积极性。在隐性分层教学法的实践中,教师根据不同层次的学生制定不同的教学目标和教学方法,为每个学生提供成功的机会,使学生获得成功的体验,进而树立学习自信心。同时,教师在整个教学过程中不断给予学生的鼓励与表扬也能够激发学生的学习热情和积极性,有助于促进学生的自我发展。

合作学习理论在隐性分层教学法中也有一定体现。合作学习理论是一种通过组织学生共同学习、互相帮助、互相评价，以提高学生的学习效果和团队协作能力的教学方法。在合作学习中，学生通常被分为若干小组，每个小组中的成员在知识、技能和背景等方面存在一定的差异，这种差异为小组内的交流和讨论提供了丰富的资源。同时，小组内的成员也会相互支持和帮助，共同完成学习任务。在隐性分层教学法中，合作学习得到了很好的应用。教师根据学生的不同层次，将学生分配到不同的学习小组中，并为每个小组设计不同的学习任务和目标。每个小组的成员都可以根据自己的能力和兴趣选择适合自己的任务，并在小组内相互学习、相互帮助。通过小组间的交流和讨论，不同层次的学生也可以相互启发、相互借鉴，从而实现共同进步。

掌握学习理论对隐性分层教学法的形成也有一定影响。掌握学习理论认为，绝大多数学生能够掌握教师所教授的事物，教学的任务就是找到使学生掌握所学学科的手段。因此，教师需要为不同层次的学生提供个性化的指导，确保他们能够掌握和理解所学内容。隐性分层教学法强调课前预习、课堂教学和课后复习三个环节的落实，保证学生达到《义务教育英语课程标准（2022年版）》（以下简称“课程标准”）规定的教学目标。在课堂教学中，教师针对不同层次的学生采用不同的教学方法和手段，使每个学生都能掌握课程标准规定的课程内容。

## 二、核心概念

隐性分层。“隐性分层”是指教育者在课堂教学过程中，根据学生的知识、能力、水平等个体差异，将学生分成不同的层次或小组，并采用不同的教学方法和评价标准，以满足不同学生的需求，促进学生的个性化发展。这种分层通常不公开或不明显，以免给学生带来心理压力或影响教学效果。

隐性分层教学法。隐性分层教学法是一种在课堂教学中关注学生个体差异，根据不同层次学生的知识水平和接受能力，制定不同层次的教学目标，采用不同层次的教学方法和手段，以使各个层次的学生都能得到充分发展的教学方法。这种教学方法的“隐性”体现为它不公开学生的层次划分，而是通过分层指导、分层练习、分层评价等环节，实现促进各层次学生整体提高、发展特长、共同进步的目的。这种教学方法也充分体现了因材施教、面向全体、主动发展的教学原则,能够有效地提高课堂教学质量。

隐形分层教学法的优点在于它能够更好地满足不同学生的学习需求,增强他们的学习效果和自信心,同时也有助于提高教师的专业水平和教学能力。隐性分层教学法应用于初中英语课堂教学,应遵循以下基本原则:

①尊重学生个体差异,实施个性化教学;②保证分层隐性,动态调整教学计划;③鼓励合作与交流,促进团队精神培养;④关注情感教育,了解学生的感受和想法。

## 三、积极作用

隐性分层教学法在初中英语写作教学中的积极作用主要体现为能够针对不同层次的学生进行教学,在保护学生自尊心的同时,增强学生的自信心,提高学生的参与度,满足学生的个性化需求,提高学生的写作质量和写作兴趣,具体表现在以下方面:

满足不同层次学生的学习需求。为了使每个层次学生的需求都能在初中英语写作教学中得到满足,教师要根据不同层次的学生来确定相应的教学目标。对于基础层,目标可以设定为掌握基本的语法和拼写知识;对于提高层,目标可以设定为增加词汇量和所用语法的复杂性;对于发展层,目标可以设定为提高写作技巧和培养批判性思维。提供个性化教学内容也是满足学生需求的一个必要条件。对于基础层,教师可以帮助他们反复练习基本语法和词汇;对于提高层,教师可以引入一些复杂的阅读材料,并指导他们从中提取信息;对于发展层,教师可以引导他们讨论更广泛的主题,以增大他们的思考深度和提高语言表达能力。作业设计分层也很重要。对于基础层,作业应以基础的语法和词汇练习为主,例如人称代词主格、宾格、所有格的练习,以及第三人称谓语动词单数形式练习等;对于提高层,作业中可以引入一些简单的造句任务,如“I love you.”这类“主+谓+宾”句或“I am a student.”这类“主+系+表”句的训练;对于发展层,教师可以布置一些需要学生深度思考和做出创造性表达的作业,如读后续写这类具有挑战性的作业。通过教学目标、教学内容、作业这三个方面的设计差异,教师可以确保每个层次的学生都能在初中英语写作教学中得到重视和进步,从而提高学生的写作水平和参与度。

增强学生的学习积极性和自信心。对于英语水平较高的学生，他们可以用更高层次的学习内容和学习方法来挑战自己，提高自己的英语能力。例如，发展层的学生可以在写作中挑战性地使用非限制性定语从句、名词性从句、强调句、倒装句等，从中感受到高级句型的语言之美。同样地，提高层和基础层的学生也能够运用教师提供的适合该层次的学习内容和方法来提高自己的能力与水平。学生可以在适合自己水平的练习中逐渐进步，从而增强自己的学习积极性和自信心。

优化教学效果。在隐性分层教学法应用于初中英语写作教学的过程中，为了优化教学效果，使教学更具有针对性和实效性，教师至少要做到课前分层准备。在充分了解每个学生能力、喜好、个性的基础上，教师设计不同的写作主题、难度和要求，然后准备不同的写作任务和指导方案。这些有针对性的举措能帮助学生取得进步，从而使教学效果得到优化。

促进学生的个性化发展。隐性分层教学法尊重学生的个体差异，鼓励学生发挥自己的优势和特长，有利于学生的个性化发展。也就是说，教师在了解学生的基础上，制订个性化的教学计划，通过设置问题、布置任务、提供资源等方式，引导学生自主探究，从而培养他们的独立思考能力和解决问题的能力。

减轻学生的学习压力。在隐性分层教学法应用于初中英语写作教学的过程中，学生的竞争压力和自我认同压力相对较小，学习压力也会相应减少。在这样的环境下，学生可能会在写作方面展现出一些出乎教师意料的提高与进步。首先，学生的写作兴趣有所提高，积极性有所增强。在压力较小的情况下，学生可能会更加享受写作过程，更加积极地参与课堂讨论和写作练习。这种积极的态度和兴趣可能会激发他们的写作热情，使他们更加愿意尝试新的写作技巧和方法。其次，学生的写作自信心会增强。学生可能会更加自信地表达自己的想法和观点。他们可能会更加勇敢地尝试新的语法、词汇和表达方式，而不太担心出错或受到批评。这种自信心的增强可能会帮助学生拥有更好的写作表现。与此同时，学生的写作技能会有所提升。他们可能会更加关注语法、词汇、句型和篇章结构等方面的练习，从而不断提高自己的写作水平。另外，学生的写作内容会得到丰富和创新。在压力较小的情况下，学生可能会更加自由地表达自己的想法和情感，从而写出更加多样化和有创意的作文。他们可能会尝试不同的写作风格和文体，探索不同的主题和观点，从而拓宽自己的写作视野。

最后,学生合作学习和交流的能力会有所提高。他们可能会组建小组,共同讨论和写出作文,互相帮助和分享经验。这种合作学习的环境会提高学生的交流与合作能力,使学生能够更好地表达自己的观点和想法。

## 第二节　隐性分层教学法可能面临的挑战与创造性解决方案

### 一、教师所面临的挑战

在实施隐性分层教学法时,教师所面临的挑战是不可忽视的,主要有以下几个方面:

理解和适应不同学生的需求。学生个体存在接受能力、学习习惯、兴趣爱好等方面的差异。为了实现隐性分层,教师需要深入了解和理解每届新生的个体差异,并在教学方法、课程设置、课后辅导等方面不断更新。教师必须在尊重学生的个体差异的基础上,鼓励学生表达自己的需求和困惑,并及时给予支持和帮助。教师必须清醒意识到与时俱进的重要性,不断更新自己、提高自己、悦纳自己,不断学习新的教学策略和方法,以应对不同层次学生的需求。教师应该经常性地参加专业发展课程和研讨会,与同行交流经验,适度提高教师的专业水平。教师也可以鼓励水平相当的学生组成小组,促使学生相互学习、交流和帮助,培养学生的合作精神和自主学习能力。

课堂管理。实施隐性分层教学法通常涉及不同层次的学生在同一班级中的学习,这对课堂管理提出了挑战。教师需要维持课堂秩序,避免因学生之间能力差距过大而产生问题。因为在教师维持课堂秩序时,学生之间能力差距过大可能会使教学内容难以满足所有学生的需求:对于能力较强的学生,如果教学内容过于简单,他们可能会觉得无聊或者无法在课堂上获得足够的挑战;而对于能力较弱的学生,他们可能无法理解或掌握具有一定难度的教学内容,导致学习效果不佳。此外,学生之间能力差距过大可能会使良好的课堂氛围难以保证:对于能力较强的学生,他们可能更愿意在课堂上参与较高难度的讨论和活动;而对于能力较弱的学生,他们可能会觉得压力较大,不愿意参与课堂活动,导致课堂氛围变得沉闷或紧张。

学生的学习动机。学习动机是激发并维持学习行为的重要心理因素,它驱动学习者参与学习过程,并为学习成果寻求积极反馈。同一个班里,学生的学习动机差异很大。一些学习能力相对较弱的学生可能会觉得自己无法跟上其他同学的进度或无法达到其他同学的水平,这会打击他们的自信心,进而削弱他们的学习动机。为此,教师首先要理解学生是有差异的。作为课堂写作学习的引导者,教师只有了解每个学生的学习动机的来源,理解他们的学习期待、兴趣、困难和优势,才能进行适当的引导。对于那些对英语写作有积极态度、对英语学习有强烈渴望的学生,教师可以鼓励他们挑战更高难度的任务;对于那些学习动机相对较弱的学生,教师应注重激发他们的学习兴趣,让他们在成功的体验中增强自信心。教师应在实践中不断创新,使用互动式教学方法、游戏化学习、虚拟现实技术等,吸引学生的注意力,激发他们的好奇心。教师要努力创造一个积极的、支持性的学习环境,使学生能够感到安全、受到尊重,从而强化学生的学习动机。

教师负担。因课堂管理和教学进度产生的连锁效应,教师的工作负担自然有所增加。教师可能需要花费更多的时间和精力来适应不同水平的学生、准备不同的教学内容和方法,这会增加教师的工作负担。如何做到既能减轻教师负担,又能提高学生的英语写作水平?首先,合理规划教学任务。根据学生的实际水平,教师可以合理规划每个层次的教学任务。对于不同层次的学生,教师可以设置相应难度的写作任务,确保学生在其能力范围内能够完成任务并获得成就感,同时也避免了过于简单或过于复杂的任务给学生带来困扰。其次,合理利用教学资源。教学软件、网络资源等现代化工具可以为学生提供多样化的写作材料和练习方式。合理利用这些工具不仅能够减轻教师批改和反馈的工作量,而且能够帮助学生用多种方法提高写作能力。最后,合理优化教学过程。教师在教学过程中应该不断总结经验,优化教学策略,提高教学效率。对于写作水平较高的学生,教师可以更多地引导他们关注写作的深层次内容;对于写作水平较低的学生,教师可以更多地引导他们关注基础语法和词汇的掌握。借助上述三个“合理”机制,教师可以在应用隐性分层教学法的同时减轻负担,更好地关注到每个学生的学习需求,增强教学效果。

## 二、学生所面临的挑战

适应新的教学方式。隐性分层教学法通常意味着教师会根据学生的能力、兴趣和背景进行分组，这可能会使学生需要适应新的教学方式和学习伙伴，继而面对一些新的挑战。在此情况下，教师可以引导学生养成做好课前准备工作这一习惯，鼓励学生对将要学习的内容进行预习，了解自己的薄弱点，以便在学习过程中有针对性地学习和改善。与此同时，学生可以在教师的引导下，对新事物保持开放心态，接受并理解不同的教学方式和学习方法，参与小组讨论并积极发言，采纳别人的不同观点，了解其他同学的想法，这有助于提高自己的沟通和协作能力，同时也有助于理解不同的观点和看法。另外，英语写作中必有困难，如果学生在学习过程中遇到困难，教师要鼓励学生不要害怕，而要鼓起勇气寻求他人的帮助。尽管适应新的教学方式需要面对挑战，但英语写作就是享受这个应对挑战、取得成功的过程。

竞争与合作。分层教学可能会引入竞争，尤其是在不同层次之间。一些学生可能会感受到压力，因为他们必须在更高的层次上保持他们的位置。同时，他们也可能会发现他们需要与他们通常不交往的学生进行合作。实际上，学生处理这种既有竞争又有合作的挑战的能力是非常重要的，而教师的参与是必要的。教师可以通过组织小组讨论、合作学习等方式，来培养学生的团队精神和合作意识。这有助于他们理解——尽管他们可能在某些方面存在竞争，但在学习、互动和合作中，他们是一个团队。培养团队精神和合作意识也能帮助学生客观公正地处理竞争与合作的关系。

自我认同和自尊心。自我认同是一个人对自己的认知和感受，包括对自己的身份、特质、价值观、目标等方面的理解和认同。自我认同是一个人心理健康的重要标志，也是一个人成长和发展中不可或缺的元素，它需要个人不断地反思、调整和探索，以适应自己和环境的变化。隐性分层教学法应用于初中英语写作教学中时，学生可能会担心他们的表现被其他学生误解，导致他们对自己产生不良看法，学生面临自我认同和自尊心被伤害的挑战。那么师生应该如何应对这个挑战呢？首先，培养学生的自我肯定语言。教师给予学生明确的写作指导并传授学生一些自我肯定的话语，如“我一直在进步”“我写得很好”“这次虽然不够完美，但下次我一定要写出自己满意的作文”等，让学生在写作过程中进行自我激励。其次,师生关系要互信、融洽。教师要与学生建立真诚的互动关系,倾听他们的担忧,并表达对他们感受的理解,让学生能感到自己被接纳和尊重,从而更愿意参与课堂活动。最后,让学生体验获得感,提供个性化反馈。当学生写作表现出色或优秀时,教师要及时给予积极的反馈和奖励,以增强学生的积极体验,使学生减少对失败的担忧。教师要给予个性化反馈,明确指出学生的优点和需要改进的地方,避免直接批评。这样有利于逐步树立学生的自信心和自我认同感,引导学生相信自己的能力,并对自己的努力感到自豪。

## 三、家长所面临的挑战

隐性分层教学法应用于初中英语写作教学,不仅给教师和学生带来挑战,给家长带来的挑战也不可忽视。各层次的学生家长面临着不同的挑战。

基础层学生的家长面临的较大挑战主要有以下三个。首先,理解和接受隐性分层教学法。家长需要理解这种教学方法的原理和目标,以便更好地配合教师完成教学任务。其次,关注孩子的进步。在隐性分层教学法的实施过程中,家长更加需要关注孩子的进步,因为他们可能无法直接看到孩子的学习进度。最后,提供必要的支持和帮助。家长需要提供必要的支持和帮助,如提供学习资源、监督孩子的学习过程、为孩子创造一个轻松愉快的学习环境、自己对孩子的写作目标也进行合理分层等。

与基础层学生的家长略有不同,提高层学生的家长面临的较大挑战是洞悉孩子的动态需求。提高层的学生通常想实现较多的更高水平的学习目标,同时需要巩固已经掌握的知识。在此情况下,家长们需要及时了解孩子的学习进度和需要,以便提供动态的、适宜的支持与帮助。

发展层学生的家长也并非"高枕无忧",他们所面临的较大挑战是保持孩子的写作热情。热情可以激发学生的学习动力和兴趣,使他们更愿意参与英语写作活动,并积极尝试不同的写作风格和表达方式。当学生对英语写作充满热情时,他们会更加关注写作的过程和结果,并努力提高自己的写作水平。此外,热情还可以增强学生的自信心和自尊心,使他们更有信心面对写作中的挑战和困难。因此,培养并保持学生对英语写作的热情是提高初中学生英语写作水平的关键之一。对于这个问题,发展层学生的家长不可忽视,应该尽己所能地提供有效的学习资源和机会,来帮助孩子提高对英语写作的热情,激励孩子保持对英语写作的兴趣和动力，确保孩子能够充分发展他们的写作技能和潜力。

## 四、隐性分层教学法所面临挑战的创造性解决方案

如前所述，隐性分层教学法应用于初中英语写作教学时，教师、学生、家长都会面临一系列挑战。那么，对于这些挑战，我们需要利用智慧提出创造性解决方案。

### （一）与家长建立伙伴关系

教师应当定期与家长进行沟通，共同讨论学生在学习方面取得的进步。教师可以努力与家长建立一种伙伴关系，使家长更支持英语写作的隐性分层教学。在隐性分层教学法应用于初中英语写作教学的情况下，教师与家长建立伙伴关系的创新方案可以归纳为以下几点：

组织家长培训并定期开展交流会。学校可以组织专门的家长培训，让教师向家长解释隐性分层教学法的理念、目的和实施方法。教师要向家长介绍英语写作在英语学习中的重要性，以及如何在家中协助孩子提高英语写作技能。定期开展家长-教师交流会，能够让教师和家长就学生在写作方面的进步和困难进行直接交流。教师和家长可以在交流会上共同讨论教学方案。

在常用的社交平台建立聊天群组。教师可以在各大常用社交平台与家长建立有针对性的聊天群组，以便家长之间随时就孩子的学习情况展开交流，更有效地解决遇到的问题。教师也可以在群内提供及时的指导。

设立家长-教师合作项目。教师可以与家长共同设计一些合作项目，如英语写作比赛，鼓励学生积极参与，在确定主题、准备比赛的过程中增强与家长之间的联系。

建立激励机制。学校或班级可以设立一些奖励机制，如优秀作文展示、进步奖等，以激发学生的写作热情，同时也能增强家长和教师对隐性分层教学法的信心。

### （二）保持学生的积极性

对于可能因分层而感到受挫的学生，教师需要特别关注，确保他们感到被接纳和理解。教师可以通过定期的鼓励和赞扬来增强学生的自信心，让他们明

白分层教学是为了有针对性地帮助他们提高英语写作水平,而不是排斥他们或将他们拒于学习门外。在初中英语写作教学中,应用隐性分层教学法,并让学生保持写作积极性的方法包括以下几点:

评估和分层。首先,教师需要对学生的英语写作水平进行评估,并根据评估结果将学生分为不同的层次。这些层次的根据是学生个体的语言能力、词汇量、语法知识和写作技巧。

制订教学计划。针对每个层次的学生,教师需要制订相应的教学计划。对于较高层次的学生,教学计划应侧重于提高他们的写作技巧和使用复杂表达的能力;对于中等层次的学生,教学计划应注重增加他们的基本语言知识和培养他们的语言学习技能;对于较低层次的学生,教学计划应侧重于基础语言技能的训练和词汇量的增加。

多元化的评估方式。教师需要采用多元化的评估方式,包括学生自评(尽量说自己的优点)、同伴互评(发展层点评提高层和基础层时,以鼓励为主;基础层和提高层点评发展层时,以学生写作亮点为着力点)和教师点评(教师点评以鼓励为主)。这样可以帮助学生更好地理解自己的写作水平,发现自己的不足,同时也能增强学生的积极性和提高学生的参与度。

定期的反馈和调整。教师需要定期对学生的写作进行反馈,并针对学生的问题进行指导。反馈的形式多种多样,具有创造性的反馈应包含面批学生习作,在指出错误的同时带着关爱的情感给予学生当面表扬。教师可以摘出学生习作的亮点,在班里展示出来,在全班学生面前表扬该生的写作亮点。此外,教师也需要根据学生的进步情况对教学计划进行调整,以适应每个学生的需求。

激发学生的兴趣。教师可以采用多种教学方法,如小组讨论、角色扮演、故事接龙等。在条件允许或征得家长、学校同意的情况下,教师可以将英语写作课搬到校外,让学生接近大自然,写出关于“自然(nature)”的书面表达。类似的这种教学方法能激发学生的学习兴趣,调动学生的写作内驱力,提高学生的写作热情,从而有效地推动学生取得进步。

创造成功的机会。教师可以设计一些具有挑战性的写作任务,让每个层次的学生都有机会尝试并成功完成。这不仅可以增强学生的自信心,也能让他们看到自己的进步,从而保持写作的积极性。

通过上述方法，隐性分层教学法可以更好地满足不同层次学生的需求，激发和维护好他们的写作积极性，从而提高他们的英语写作能力。

(三)利用技术工具

教师可以利用一些技术工具，如在线学习平台，来跟踪学生的学习进度和成绩。家长也可以通过这些在线学习平台了解和理解教师是如何使用隐性分层教学法的。

创建个人在线账户。教师可以为每个学生家长创建一个独立的在线账户，便于追踪孩子的学习进度和成绩，同时要倡导家长之间互相保密，不外露学生成绩。

设定目标。在每次写作课程开始时，教师应与学生讨论并设定明确的目标。这些目标应与他们的英语水平、兴趣和即将到来的考试相关。

记录反馈。每次学生提交作文后，教师应给予及时反馈，包括语法、拼写、结构等方面的建议。在线平台的优点是可以快速提供大量反馈，让学生能同时看到自己的优点和需要改进的地方。

进度跟踪。在线平台通常具有跟踪学生完成度、活跃度、作业质量水平等功能，这有助于教师了解学生的学习进度。教师和家长随时随地可以查看学生的学习过程和作业完成度。

成绩评估。定期评估学生的写作成绩有助于追踪他们的进步。在线平台的另一个优点是能轻松地生成成绩报告，使教师更容易知晓学生的表现。

共享资源。利用在线平台的资源库，教师可以定期或不定期地分享高质量的英语写作文章和练习，以扩展学生的阅读和写作材料。

设立讨论专区。教师可以设立在线讨论区，供学生提问、分享想法和讨论写作主题。这不仅可以提高学生的参与度，还能提供一个交流和反馈的平台。

数据分析。教师可以利用在线平台的统计功能，分析学生的学习数据，以便更好地了解他们的学习模式和弱点，进而制定更有效的教学策略。此外，教师应定期与家长分享数据，体现学生取得的进步和正在应对的挑战，说明教师正在采取的措施，这有助于建立家校合作的良好模式。

### (四)培养学生的自尊心和自信心

实施隐性分层教学法的一个重要目标是培养学生的自尊心和自信心。教师应鼓励学生,赞扬他们的努力和进步,让他们明白他们的努力得到了认可。在初中英语写作教学中,教师可以使用以下方法来培养学生的自尊心和自信心:

分层评估。根据学生的写作水平进行分层,并为每一层设立不同的评估标准。对于较低层次的学生,重点在于鼓励他们尝试并给予建设性的反馈;而对于较高层次的学生,则更应注重在内容深度和准确性方面的反馈。这种方式可以让学生看到自己的进步,增强他们的自信心。

个性化辅导。教师应针对每个层次的学生提供个性化的写作指导。对于较低层次的学生,可以通过对基础语法和词汇知识的讲解来帮助他们;对于较高层次的学生,可以提供更复杂的关于写作技巧和策略的指导。

同伴互评。"兵教兵"的做法虽然传统,但也具有一定意义。教师可以鼓励学生互相评价和提出修改建议,这不仅可以提高他们的批判性思维能力,还可以让他们从其他同学的反馈中获得有价值的信息。教师可以在此过程中给予监督和指导,确保公平和尊重。

创造性的反馈。反馈应以鼓励和赞扬为主,尽量避免批评。对于学生的每一点进步,无论是大还是小,教师都应给予肯定。此外,可以通过小故事、小贴士等形式提供反馈,使反馈更具有趣味性和启发性。

创造性的写作任务。教师可以设计不同层次、不同主题的写作任务,以满足不同学生的需求。比如,设计一些具有挑战性的任务,让较高层次的学生发挥自身能力;设计一些较容易的任务,让较低层次的学生因成功完成任务而增强信心。

课堂外的写作练习。教师应鼓励学生利用课外时间进行写作练习,如日记、书信、故事创作等。这种方式不仅可以提高学生的写作技能,还可以培养他们的自主学习能力。教师需要保持耐心和理解,允许学生有进步缓慢期。教师要不急不躁,不让任何一个学生掉队,培养学生的自尊心和自信心,提高他们的英语写作能力。

## 第三节　隐性分层教学法的实际应用

教师根据学生的英语水平,将学生大致分为基础层、提高层、发展层,再针对不同层次的学生,设计不同难度和要求的写作任务,以便更好地适应不同学生的需求。教师可以综合以下三方面的情况将学生分层。首先,课堂观察和交流是较为直观的分层依据。教师可以根据学生平时在课堂上的表现和交流情况,判断他们在英语写作方面的能力和水平,进而将学生分成不同的层次。其次,成绩评价也是隐性分层的一个渠道。教师可以将学生每周一练的英语写作成绩作为分层的一个参考因素。通过对学生平时的写作情况的评估,教师可以大致判断出学生的写作水平,进而将其归入相应的层次。最后,通过作业情况进行研判。初中生英语写作作业研判对教师和学生来说都是非常重要的。教师可以根据学生英语写作作业的完成情况来判断他们的写作水平。需要注意的是,在进行隐性分层的过程中,教师需要注意保护学生的自尊心,避免公开告知学生分层情况,以免给学生带来不必要的心理压力。

通过以上方法对学生进行隐性分层后,教师可以有针对性地设定教学目标、教学内容、教学方法与评价方式,具体如表 1.1 所示:

表 1.1　隐性分层教学法针对各层次的教学目标、教学内容、教学方法与评价方式

| 层次 | 教学目标 | 教学内容 | 教学方法 | 评价方式 |
|---|---|---|---|---|
| 基础层 | 掌握基本词汇和语法结构 | 强化词汇和语法学习,提供简单的写作练习 | 讲解+示范+模仿+反馈 | 纠错为辅,鼓励为主 |
| 提高层 | 运用高级词汇和语法结构,表达较为复杂的观点 | 提供中等难度的写作练习,加强写作技巧训练 | 小组讨论+个人创作+反馈指导 | 注重进步,鼓励创新 |
| 发展层 | 注重文章的结构和逻辑性,表达自己的独特见解 | 提供具有挑战性的写作主题,培养思维能力和表达能力 | 个人创作+反馈指导+点评交流 | 表扬为主,鼓励创新和挑战 |

完成隐性分层后，教师应及时开展写作指导，以帮助学生在写作过程中更好地组织思路和表达思想。教师应在写作指导阶段针对不同层次的学生采用不同的指导方式。

针对基础层的学生，教师应着重强化他们的基础知识，包括词汇、语法和基本句型。教师可以安排专门的辅导时间，帮助他们理解和记忆这些基础知识，例如，记忆以 f/fe 结尾的名词变复数时需要把 f/fe 变为 ves 的单词时，可以编成顺口溜：妻子（wife）拿着刀子（knife）去宰狼（wolf），吓得小偷（thief）发了慌，躲在架（shelf）后保己（self）命（life），半（half）片树叶（leaf）遮目光。这样的顺口溜简单易懂、方便记忆，基础层学生很喜爱。教师要帮助基础层学生选择合适的词汇、表达方式、文章结构，采取个性化的专项辅导。对于语法错误较多的学生，可以专门进行语法训练；对于词汇量不足的学生，可以提供额外的词汇学习资料。教师要确保实现写作技巧与个性化辅导的紧密结合。

对于提高层的学生，教师应注重写作技巧的培训。段落构建能力的培训不可缺少，学会构建一个有逻辑、有层次的段落对提高层的学生来说至关重要：用一个主题句开始，然后通过几个支持性的细节进行扩展，最后以一个结论句结束。对于提高层的学生来说，针对作文结构的训练需要经常化，教师要指导他们设计一个清晰的文章结构，包括引言、主体和结论，写出具有简单、明了的语言风格的作文。足够的写作训练对于提高学生的写作水平至关重要。教师要给学生创造足够的写作机会，提供足够的写作练习，让他们在实际语境中应用所学知识。教师可以布置定期的写作任务，让学生在规定的时间内完成，并给予及时的反馈。文章质量的优劣取决于对所写作文的纠错是否完美，培养提高层学生的纠错和改进能力，有助于优化他们的写作水平。对于初级错误，如拼写和标点符号错误，应要求他们及时纠正。对于一些常见错误，可以集体讲解，让他们在作业本上反复修改，以避免在写作中再次犯错。教师也应引导学生学习如何进行自我评估和反思，以便他们能够了解自己的进步并找出可以改进的地方。教师也要布置一些有趣的写作主题和活动来激发学生的写作兴趣，让他们更愿意投入到写作中。另外，教师要鼓励提高层的学生与其他层次的学生合作学习，互相交流和分享写作经验，从而不断提高他们的写作技巧。

对于发展层的学生，教师要注重写作深度的拓展和写作风格的指导。发展层学生基础扎实，技能训练有素，教师要为他们设立更高层次的写作目标。这些目标可以包括复杂句式的使用、对主题的深入探讨,以及在写作中体现独特的个人风格。通常来看,课堂写作对发展层学生来说“吃不饱”,所以为发展层提供额外的写作辅导是必要的。教师应帮助他们深入挖掘主题,引导他们探讨更深层次的观点,也可以提供一些关于写作风格和表达技巧的额外指导。三人行,必有我师焉。通过开展发展层学生之间的交流与沟通,发展层学生可以获得更多的灵感和启示,从而有助于拓展写作深度。在日常教学中,不论对于哪个层次的学生,教师都会展示一些优秀的范文,让学生从中汲取营养。发展层也不例外。教师可以让发展层分析一些优秀的英语范文,引导他们从中学习写作技巧、表达方式、深度话题的探讨角度等,从而不断完善自己的作文。在课内及课外,教师都鼓励学生提高创新迁移能力,发展层更需要得到鼓励,从而在写作上大胆创新。教师要鼓励他们在写作中尝试使用新的句式和词汇,以形成自己的独特风格。同时,教师要引导他们尊重并学习其他学生的优点以取长补短。此外,教师的写后反馈必不可少。教师应及时给予学生反馈,包括写作任务的完成情况、写作技巧的应用情况以及需要改进的地方等。发展层学生的作文不可能一直保持较高水准,肯定会存在质量波动的时候,因此,教师对发展层也要进行动态管理,根据学生的写作情况适时调整学生的层次。这种动态的管理方式可以激励学生不断进步。例如,对于“毫无疑问,这本书是她的”这句话,基础层只要写出“This book belongs to her.”即可,但是提高层写出“The book belongs to her without doubt.”的大有人在;而发展层一般会想到使用同位语从句,写出“There is no doubt that this book belongs to her.”。假如提高层中有写出这种好句子的学生,那么他/她的进步需要得到肯定和表扬。教师可以将该句在班级里公开展示,让其他学生为写出该句的学生鼓掌,并将写出该句的学生隐性分层到发展层,这种动态管理有助于学生信心的增强和写作能力的进步。

## 第四节　隐性分层教学法应用于初中英语写作教学中的具体步骤

隐性分层教学法应用于初中英语写作教学中的具体步骤应该至少包括以

下几个方面：

## 一、写作任务准备

教师在使用隐性分层教学法时，需要准备针对不同层次的写作任务，以满足不同层次学生的需求：

基础层。对于基础较弱的学生，教师可以准备一些简单的写作任务，如用简单的词汇和语法表达观点、描述图片等。写作任务应相对简单、易于理解，如 Introduce My Family。对于这样的简单写作，基础层的学生都能写出“I have a happy family. There is a kind father. There is a beautiful mother. I have a naughty brother. I love my family.”诸如此类的简单明了的句子。这些句子可以让基础层的学生较少犯错误，有利于基础层学生增强写作信心。

提高层。对于中等水平的学生，教师可以准备一些有一定难度的写作任务，如要求学生对某个话题进行论述。教师可以提供一些复杂的词汇和语法结构。写作任务虽具有一定的挑战性，但仍然在学生的理解范围内，例如：写邮件、通知、便条等，这类写作任务相对简单，但可以帮助学生提高语言运用能力；描述一个场景、一个人或事物，这类写作任务可以帮助学生提高描述能力和细节描写能力；分析一个观点、问题或现象等，这类写作任务可以帮助学生提高分析问题和表达观点的能力；编写故事、诗歌或剧本等，这类写作任务可以激发学生的想象力和创造力，使作文内容生动有趣；根据要求完成一篇短文或对话，这类写作任务可以帮助学生提高语言组织和表达能力。除了在写作任务方面设置一定的挑战外，教师还可以为提高层准备一些具有挑战性的复杂句，让学生学会将这些句子运用到写作之中：用并列连词如 and、but、or 连接句子，见例句“I like to read books and I can also play the piano.”；用关联词如 when、where、why 等引导从句，见例句“When I finish my homework, I can play video games.”；比较两个或多个事物之间的相似或不同之处的比较句，见例句“Our teacher is much more patient than our principal.”；使用复杂的主语、宾语、状语等，或者使用复杂句型结构如强调、倒装等，见例句“Unless you work hard, or you won't succeed/be successful.”等；使用“it's+adj. +for/of sb. to do sth.”“it's +adj. /n. +that+clause”等 it 做形式主语的高级句型，见例句“It's kind of you to help me.”。

发展层。对于发展层的学生，教师可以准备一些更高难度的写作任务，如要求学生对某个复杂的问题进行分析,或者使用一些高级的词汇和语法结构。写作任务应具有更高的挑战性,以提高他们的创造力和思考能力。教师可以考虑布置以下写作任务。①主题讨论。教师可以选择一些开放性的主题,如"环保""未来科技"等,让学生根据自身观点进行写作。这种主题能激发学生的想象力,引导他们运用高级词汇和句型来表达观点。②互动写作。教师可以设计一些互动式的写作任务,如小组讨论后撰写报告,或给定一个情境让小组内部进行角色扮演后做出书面报告。这样的任务可以培养学生的团队合作和沟通交流能力,也能提高他们的写作技巧。③范文分析。教师可以提供一些优秀的英语范文,让学生分析其中的高级词汇、语法及写作技巧,之后让学生模仿这些范文进行写作,帮助学生提高写作水平。④英汉翻译练习。教师可以布置一些难度较高的英汉翻译练习,让学生在翻译过程中学习并运用高级词汇和语法,同时积累一些地道的表达方式。⑤词汇扩展。教师还可以准备一些难度较高的词汇,让学生根据上下文进行理解和运用。这样既可以提高他们的思考能力,又可以锻炼学生的词汇运用能力。除了上述写作任务,教师还应鼓励批判性思考。优秀的学生往往对知识有更深层次的理解和探索欲望。教师可以通过引导学生进行批判性思考,鼓励他们从多角度分析问题,进一步提高他们的创新能力。在语法结构方面,教师对发展层要给出更具挑战性的句型,如"it's+时间或地点状语+that+其他",让发展层在理解的同时学会运用高级句型,不断写出高分作文。

## 二、巧妙布置任务

在初中英语写作教学中,隐性分层教学法要求教师根据学生的英语水平和学习风格布置不同的写作任务,并给予有针对性的指导,以提高所有学生的英语写作能力。

基础层。对于基础层的学生,教师可以布置一些简单的写作任务,比如描述图片、编写故事梗概、改写短文等。在写作过程中,教师可以提供一些基本的语法和词汇帮助,并给予积极的反馈和建议,以增强学生的自信心和提高写作兴趣。

提高层。对于提高层的学生,教师可以布置一些具有挑战性的写作任务,比如编写故事、发表个人观点、仿写段落等。这些任务可以训练学生的逻辑思维和表达能力，并为学生提供更多的语法和词汇选择。在写作过程中，教师可以给予一些具体的写作技巧指导，帮助学生提高写作水平。

发展层。对于发展层的学生，教师可以布置一些更具挑战性和创造性的写作任务，比如合作写作、应用文写作等。这些任务可以培养学生的批判性思维和跨文化交际能力，并提供更多的写作风格和文体的选择。同时，教师可以给予一些更高层次的写作技巧指导，帮助学生拓宽视野和思维。

在布置写作任务时，教师必须保证任务难度适中，符合学生的实际水平和学习需求；任务内容要有趣、实用，能够激发学生的写作兴趣；任务形式要多样化，包括书面写作、口头表达、小组讨论等。通过为不同层次的学生布置不同任务，教师能够让所有学生的语言综合运用能力在英语写作中得到锻炼和提高。

## 三、关注写作过程和结果

在课堂上，学生根据教师布置的任务开始写作。在学生的写作过程中，教师必须通过跟踪学生的写作进度、关注学生的语言使用、观察学生的写作风格和习惯等方式，来关注学生的写作过程，具体来说：

跟踪学生的写作进度。教师可以通过定期查看学生的写作进度，了解他们在写作过程中遇到的困难和挑战。这可以通过课堂展示、面谈或在线反馈等方式进行。

关注学生的语言使用。教师需要关注学生在作文中使用的词汇、语法和语篇结构等。对于使用恰当词汇和复杂句型的学生，教师应给予肯定和表扬；对于使用过于基础甚至错误的、不恰当词汇和句型的学生，教师应给予及时的提示与鼓励。

观察学生的写作风格和习惯。教师通过观察学生的写作风格和习惯，如作文的组织方式、思考问题的角度等，判断这些作文是否符合英语写作的一般规律，对学生的一些不良语言习惯和错误倾向要及时纠正。

对于一些在写作中遇到困难的学生，教师可以通过以下几种方式予以帮助：针对学生在写作中遇到的词汇、语法、结构等难题进行有针对性的辅导；根据学生的写作水平和具体问题，提供个性化的反馈和建议，帮助学生明确下一步的写作方向；组织小组讨论或合作学习，让写作水平高的学生带动和帮助那些存在写作困难的学生,促进他们的交流与合作,使学生的写作能力得到共同提高;对学生的尝试和努力给予肯定和支持,帮助他们建立克服困难的信心;如果学生需要更多的资源来辅助他们的写作,教师可以提供额外的阅读材料、在线资源或课后辅导等。

学生完成写作后,教师要对他们的作文进行评价。评价时,教师应注重保护学生的自尊心,对不同层次的学生采用不同的评价标准。对于基础层的学生,评价重点在于发现他们的进步和优点;对于提高层和发展层的学生,评价应更注重他们的准确性和创新性。评价完成后,教师应及时将评价结果反馈给学生,帮助他们改进作文。针对学生出现的问题,教师可以进行个别辅导或集体讲解,使学生掌握更多的写作技巧和方法。

隐性分层教学法应用于初中英语写作教学的效果可以通过各种手段进行评估。在日常教学中,通常采用以下几种评估方式:

自我评估。教师应引导学生学会对自身作文的质量,包括语法、词汇、结构等方面的正确性和准确性进行自我评估。教师可以提供自我评估的模板和指导,帮助学生进行评估。学生可以从定性和定量两个方面实施自我写作评估,具体分别见表 1.2 和表 1.3。得到自我评估结果后,学生可以了解自己在写作方面的优势与不足,从而有针对性地做出改进、取得进步。

**表 1.2　定性评估**

| 要素 | 等级 | 具体表现 |
|---|---|---|
| 内容 | 非常好 | 能够清晰地表达自己的观点和想法,内容丰富多样。 |
|  | 较　好 | 能够表达自己的观点和想法,但内容不够丰富多样。 |
|  | 一　般 | 能够表达一些观点和想法,但需要加强练习。 |
| 语法 | 非常好 | 语法完全正确,没有错误。 |
|  | 较　好 | 语法基本正确,有些小错误。 |
|  | 一　般 | 有些语法错误,需要加强练习。 |
| 词汇量 | 非常好 | 能够使用适当的词汇来表达自己的意思,词汇量丰富。 |
|  | 较　好 | 能够使用一些适当的词汇来表达自己的意思,词汇量适中。 |
|  | 一　般 | 使用了一些词汇,但需要加强学习。 |

表 1.3 定量评估

| 要素 | 等级 | 具体表现 |
|---|---|---|
| 字数 | 完全符合 | 字数非常合适,没有超出或少于字数要求。 |
| | 基本符合 | 字数稍微超出或少于要求,但不会影响整体质量。 |
| | 不符合 | 字数明显超出或少于要求,需要重新修改。 |
| 结构 | 非常好 | 段落和结构清晰,逻辑性强。 |
| | 较 好 | 段落和结构基本清晰,但需要加强逻辑性。 |
| | 一 般 | 段落和结构不够清晰,需要重新修改。 |

反馈和讨论。教师提供反馈意见,包括语法、词汇、结构等方面的建议,学生可以根据这些反馈展开讨论,并尝试从中学到新的写作技巧和方法。教师也可以引导学生对作文展开互评,使每位学生获得他人视角下的评价和建议。教师反馈和学生讨论可分别参照表 1.4、表 1.5 来进行。教师提供的反馈和学生的讨论都应该基于对学生作文的分析和理解,并提供具体的建议和指导,以帮助受评者提高他们的英语写作水平。同时,教师应该与学生积极互动,鼓励学生对自己的作文进行反思和改进,以提高他们的写作能力和信心。

表 1.4 教师反馈

| 要素 | 具体表现 |
|---|---|
| 内容 | 教师需要检查学生的作文内容是否符合题目要求、是否具有逻辑性和连贯性。 |
| 语法 | 教师需要检查作文中的语法错误,包括时态、单复数等。对于一些常见的语法错误,教师可以提前准备一份清单,以便快速反馈给学生。 |
| 结构 | 教师需要检查作文的结构是否清晰,是否符合英语写作的规范。 |
| 词汇 | 教师需要检查作文中的词汇使用是否得当,是否能够准确表达意思。 |
| 反馈 | 教师根据上述标准对学生的作文进行反馈。反馈应该包括问题所在和改进建议,以便学生了解自己的不足并加以改进。 |

表 1.5 学生讨论

| 要素 | 具体内容 |
|---|---|
| 主题 | 讨论的主题应该围绕学生作文所涉及的内容,例如语法、词汇、结构等。 |
| 观点分享 | 学生应该分享他们对作文主题的想法,并讨论如何使用英语来表达这些想法。这将有助于提高学生的英语表达能力。 |
| 问题提出和回答 | 学生可以提出自己在写作中遇到的问题,并互相回答。这将有助于他们发现彼此的不足,并共同寻求解决方案。 |
| 讨论结果 | 讨论结束后,学生应该总结讨论中提出的问题和解决方案,并讨论下一步的行动计划。这将有助于他们了解彼此的看法,并制订和改进计划。 |

写作任务评分。教师可以制定评分标准和规则,对学生完成的写作任务进行评分。这种评估方式应当以鼓励为主,给予学生必要的反馈,帮助学生改进写作技巧和方法。初中英语写作任务的评分标准可参见表 1.6。学生作文的每一个部分都会被详细地评分,并最终综合起来得到一个总分。这个评分标准要保证客观、公正、透明。

表 1.6 初中英语写作任务评分标准

| 要素 | 评分标准 |
|---|---|
| 内容要点 | 是否包含了所有指定的内容要点,这是决定是否得分的基本点。 |
| 语言使用 | 评估语法、拼写和标点错误,以及使用的单词、词组和句式的多样性。 |
| 结构组织 | 分析文章是否有一个清晰的结构,以及所用句子的复杂程度。 |
| 语言表达的准确性 | 评估语言表达的准确性,包括单词和语法。 |
| 连贯性 | 考查句与句、段与段之间的连贯性。 |
| 总体印象 | 给分时通常会考虑文章给人的整体印象,比如篇幅、整洁度等。 |

阶段性测试。教师可以在一段时间内组织阶段性测试,检测学生的英语写作水平是否确有提高。测试可以包括不同的写作主题和难度级别,以适应不同层次的学生。阶段性测试的具体写作任务等可参见表 1.7。

表 1.7 阶段性测试

| 要素 | 具体内容 |
| --- | --- |
| 写作任务 | 基础层:侧重基础的语法和词汇使用,同时注意词性和词汇的正确形式。 |
| | 提高层:增加一些复杂的句子结构和表达方式。 |
| | 发展层:展示更深入的思考和更丰富的表达。 |
| 测试形式 | 看图写文;看表写文;根据提示自由发挥;等等。 |
| 写作主题 | 基础层:介绍一个人、一个地方或一个事件;描述一天的活动;表达对某个事物的看法;等等。 |
| | 提高层:比较两个事物或观点;讲述一个故事并说明其中的寓意;使用复杂的句子结构表达复杂的思想;等等。 |
| | 发展层:使用英语描述一个抽象概念;评价、分析一个社会现象;用英语写一份报告或论文;等等。 |
| 具体操作 | 1. 了解每个学生的现有水平,根据他们的优势和弱点进行分层。<br>2. 对于不同层次的学生,给予不同的指导和反馈,鼓励他们挑战自己,向更高一层发展。<br>3. 难度级别不是一成不变的,可以根据学生的学习进展进行适当的调整,以适应他们的需要。<br>注:在把握难度级别时,教师还需要考虑学生的英语水平和写作能力之间的匹配度。如果一个学生英语水平很高但写作能力很弱,那么他/她可能需要更多的帮助和指导来提高他/她的写作技能。相反,如果一个学生的英语水平较弱,但他/她的写作能力很强,那么他/她可能更适合完成一些需要更多创新和思考的写作任务。 |

学生互换作文。教师可以让不同层次的学生互换作文,以了解学生之间的互动和合作情况,以及不同层次的学生在写作方面的进步。学生可依据表 1.8 来对彼此的作文进行评估。通过这个量表,学生可以对彼此的作文进行客观、全面的评价,从而更好地了解自己和同伴在写作方面取得的进步。同时,这个量表的统计结果可以为教师提供隐性分层教学法在初中英语写作教学中的应用效果的参考信息。

表 1.8 学生互换作文评估

| 要素 | 措施 | 具体内容 |
| --- | --- | --- |
| 技能提升 | 学生阅读对方作文，评估对方在写作技能方面的提升情况。 | 学生可以回答以下问题：<br>• 你认为这篇作文的语法正确吗？<br>• 这篇作文的词汇量是否丰富？<br>• 这篇作文的连续性如何？ |
| 内容质量 | 学生评估对方作文的内容质量。 | 学生可以回答以下问题：<br>• 这篇作文的主题明确吗？<br>• 这篇作文是否充分表达了作者的观点？ |
| 态度与合作 | 学生评估对方在写作过程中的态度和合作情况。 | 学生可以回答以下问题：<br>• 你认为这位同学在写作过程中有足够的积极性吗？<br>• 在合作完成作文的过程中,你们是否有足够的沟通与理解？ |
| 成果展示 | 对互换作文的学习过程及学习效果进行整体评估,可以选择量化的形式展示评估结果。 | 学生可以回答以下问题：<br>• 你觉得通过互换作文的学习,你的英语写作水平是否有所提高？<br>• 你是否愿意继续接受这种教学方式？<br>• 你认为这种教学方式对其他学科的学习是否有帮助？ |

家长反馈。家长也可以参与评估,提供对学生写作表现的反馈意见。这可以帮助教师从另一个角度了解学生的需求和进步情况。通过多维度评估,教师可以全面了解隐性分层教学法在初中英语写作教学中的实际效果,从而不断调整和改进教学方法,以提高教学质量和学生的写作水平。家长可参照表 1.9 来对学生的写作表现提供反馈。通过家长参与评价和反馈,家长与学生之间的沟通和互动得到促进,家长对英语写作教学的关注和参与度也会增加。同时,通过这个量表,家长可以了解学生在不同层次的表现和进步情况,从而更加理解与支持隐性分层教学法在初中英语写作教学中的应用。

**表 1.9 家长对学生写作表现反馈**

| 写作表现评价 | 反馈意见(示例) | 鼓励与支持(示例) |
|---|---|---|
| 语法准确性 | 基础层:总体较好,但在某些句子中还需要注意时态和冠词的使用,且主谓一致问题比较突出。 | 基础层:你做得很好,继续努力! |
| | 提高层:复杂语法结构的运用比较精准,句子间语法逻辑连贯,写作中展现了一定的语法创新意识,巧妙地运用一些特殊的语法结构来实现个性化表达。但写作中存在一些语法一致性方面的问题,代词指代一致性也有欠缺。 | 提高层:你在写作中尝试运用复杂语法结构的做法非常好,这是提高语法准确性的有效途径。 |
| | 发展层:语法运用炉火纯青,语法服务于语义表达,能根据不同的写作主题和体裁调整语法的运用方式。但偶尔会出现一些拼写和标点使用不当影响语法准确性的情况,如 it's 和 its 的混淆,以及逗号、句号的错误使用导致句子结构不清晰。有时过于追求语法结构的复杂性而忽略了内容的自然流畅。 | 发展层:孩子,各种复杂的语法结构在你笔下运用得游刃有余,无论是定语从句、状语从句还是名词性从句,你在作文中的使用都精准无误,且与上下文融合得恰到好处。你的英语写作的语法准确性已经超越了很多同龄人,展现出了非凡的天赋和潜力。你对语法规则的深入理解和创新运用,让文章变得生动有趣又富有逻辑性。 |
| 拼写正确性 | 基础层:有时会出现一些小错误,从文章中可以看出你可能缺乏写完后检查拼写的意识,一些本来可以避免的错误没有被发现,但总体拼写能力不错。 | 基础层:每一个正确拼写的单词都是你努力的成果,虽然还有一些小错误,但这丝毫不能掩盖你付出的努力和取得的进步。继续保持! 加油! |
| | 提高层:处理不同词性和词形变化时,拼写非常精准,有很强的检查纠错意识,善于运用一些拼写技巧来避免错误。但对于一些含有不发音字母的单词,如 knife、debt 等,你偶尔会忽略不发音字母,导致拼写错误。 | 提高层:你善于运用各种学习技巧来提高拼写准确性,这种自主学习的能力是很多人都渴望拥有的。你的潜力是无限的,在英语拼写方面还有很大的提升空间。 |
| | 发展层:在写作中,你对各种复杂的词形变化处理得游刃有余。拼写错误率极低且有自查能力。你不仅能够发现明显的拼写错误,还能对一些容易混淆的词汇进行仔细甄别。当遇到需要进行词类转换的情况时,你也能准确地完成拼写。例如,将 create(创造)变成 creativity(创造力)、strong(强壮的)变成 strength(力量)。但也有语境干扰造成的拼写偏差,如把 desperate(绝望的)写成了 despreat。 | 发展层:你的英语写作在拼写正确性上已经达到了发展层的优秀水平,这是很多同龄人都难以企及的。虽然在个别生僻词和新学词汇的拼写方面还存在一些小问题,但这丝毫不会影响你在英语学习上的出色表现。 |

**续表**

| 写作表现评价 | 反馈意见(示例) | 鼓励与支持(示例) |
|---|---|---|
| 词汇量 | 基础层:常用词汇掌握较好,但词汇量整体较少,缺乏词汇拓展意识。 | 基础层:初步具备了用英语进行简单交流和表达的能力,很棒! |
| | 提高层:需要加强词汇积累,以提高表达的丰富性和准确性。 | 提高层:词汇是英语写作的基础,加油! |
| | 发展层:词汇丰富度高,运用精准恰当,善于使用派生词和合成词。但词汇搭配存在小瑕疵,如 make a decision 是常见的搭配,而你写成了 do a decision。 | 发展层:你的词汇储备就像丰富的宝藏,不断为你的写作提供强大的支持。每一次挑战都是一次成长的机会,加油,我看好你! |
| 结构逻辑 | 基础层:文章能体现基本结构意识,简单逻辑关系可辨,但主线不清,有些句子之间没有明显的关联。 | 基础层:你的写作已经有了一定的基础,只要再努力一把,把结构和逻辑方面的问题解决好,就能更上一层楼。 |
| | 提高层:文章结构精巧合理,逻辑严密连贯。但结构细节有瑕疵,开头和结尾部分可以再优化。 | 提高层:你在写作上已经取得了很大的进步,但是不要满足于现状哦,要不断学习新的知识和技巧。 |
| | 发展层:文章结构较清晰,但有些句子之间的衔接不够自然。 | 发展层:多练习连句成段,提高逻辑表达能力。 |
| 表达清晰度 | 基础层:词汇使用基本准确,句子结构简单清晰,整体意思能被理解。但有些句子的语序不当,信息传递不完整。 | 基础层:英语写作像滴水穿石一样,只要坚持不懈,小小的水滴也能穿透坚硬的石头,你也能写出更好更优秀的作文。 |
| | 提高层:词汇运用精准丰富,句子结构多样准确,信息传达连贯清晰。但句子过于冗长复杂,导致重点不够突出。 | 提高层:你在写作上的潜力是无限的,这次在表达清晰度上的进步只是一个开始。 |
| | 发展层:总体表达清晰,但在某些细节处需要改进。 | 发展层:继续保持清晰表达的习惯,相信你可以做得更好! |
| 使用步骤 | • 仔细阅读表中的写作表现评价和反馈意见部分,了解评价标准和具体意见。<br>• 根据学生的写作表现,给予相应评价,同时提出具体的反馈和建议。<br>• 在鼓励与支持部分,可以写下一些鼓励和支持的话语,以增强学生的自信心和写作动力。<br>• 将此表交给教师或学校相关部门,以便教师了解家长对学生写作表现的看法和建议。 | |

## 四、学生进步实例

在笔者的教学实践中，接受隐性分层教学法的学生在英语写作方面都取得了明显的进步。下面以三名同学的作文为例，展示学生在接受隐性分层教学法之后，其作文的具体进步。

首先来看第一个实例。要求学生以“My Childhood Fun Story”为题，介绍一下自己记忆最深刻的童年往事。我们一起来看教师未执行隐性分层教学时一名学生的作文(含有一定错误，仅做展示之用)：

### My Childhood Fun Story

In my childhood life, there are so many memories, but I remembered the clearest memory is a funny story. One day at five, I found a beautiful doll, this doll was playing by my sister. The doll has long blonde hair and big blue eyes. I can't stand playing it. So I hid it in my room. I was excited to hide the doll so I jumped up and down with joy. Because I made noise, my mom came into to see what happened. She was angry when she saw the doll. There was an angry face on her and let me give the doll back to my sister. I wanted to explain it but there was no understand for me. To my joy, mom didn't hit me.

Now the moment I remember the event, I laugh at myself for my naughty. I think my mom was a kind and understand person, because she didn't harm me. I think it was a small thing, but it was one of the best memories. I will never forget.

作者在本文中写下了一件童年趣事——偷藏妹妹的玩具。叙述内容基本清楚，但是语言错误较多，例如，“I wanted to explain it but there was no understand for me.”中的错误非常明显，可见作者在understand与understanding的词性记忆与使用方面还是存在偏差。不过，作者对there be句型的运用比较正确，值得表扬。除了语言错误外，过渡语言较少也是这篇作文的缺点，这使整体的逻辑性受到了很大影响。尽管这篇作文存在许多问题，但有很大的进步空间，只要通过隐性分层教学法指导，作者的写作水平肯定会有所提高。

这篇作文的作者小刘是一个英语水平中等的学生。在了解小刘的英语写作水平之后，老师采取了隐性分层教学法的个性化辅导方式，为小刘安排了单独的语法和词汇训练。经过老师的指导,小刘能成功地运用所学到的记叙文写作技巧进行写作,包括如何设置故事背景、人物角色、情节发展等。他所写的文章生动有趣,语言表达流畅,情感表达真实,得到了老师和同学们的赞赏。一年后,他仍然以“My Childhood Fun Story”为题,写了一篇英语作文。老师将他的作文展示在希沃白板上,供大家赏析。在老师的授意下,年级第一名小郑对该文做了精彩的点评。小郑同学认为:小刘同学这篇记叙文主题明确,主要讲述了作者童年时与妹妹的玩具相关的趣事,回忆部分内容丰富且充满感情,叙事流畅,情节转折自然,对具体场景和人物动作的描绘生动形象,让读者有代入感。小刘通过回忆表现出自己的成长和反思,这是文章的一大亮点。另外,作文中语言表达准确,语法正确,用词恰当,没有明显的语言错误。当然,小刘同学这篇作文并非完美无缺,缺点主要体现为描述自己母亲的反应时过于简略,如果能更详细地描述母亲的表情和语气,可能会使读者更好地理解作者当时的尴尬和困惑。下文是小刘接受隐性分层教学之后写出的文章,画线部分是可供学生赏析和学习的内容。

### My Childhood Fun Story

When I think back on my childhood, memories come flooding in. There were so many wonderful moments that I've shared with my family and friends, but one of my most precious ones is a funny story that I still remember clearly today.

When I was around five years old, I used to love playing with my sister's toys. One day, I found a beautiful doll that she had been playing with. It had long blonde hair and big blue eyes, and I couldn't resist taking it for myself. I decided to hide the doll in my room, and I was so excited about my secret hiding place that I couldn't keep my excitement to myself. I started jumping up and down and yelling with joy, waking up my whole family. My mother came into my room to see what was going on, and when she saw the doll, she was not pleased. She scolded me for being naughty and told me to give the doll back to my sister immediately. I tried to explain that I had hidden it so that she wouldn't find it, but my mother didn't seem to understand.

Looking back on that day, I laugh at myself for being so naughty and forgetting that my mother was a kind and understanding person who would never harm me.

Although it was a silly thing to do, it's one of the best memories I have from my childhood. So, if you ask me about my most memorable childhood story, this is the one that comes to mind. It may not seem like much to some people, but it holds a special place in my heart because it reminds me of all the fun and carefree days of my childhood.

在这篇作文中,作者通过具体的事例和生动的描述,让读者能够身临其境般地感受到作者童年的快乐和无忧无虑。作者在描述自己的行为和母亲的反应时,使用了恰当的词语和句型,表达清晰准确。作者在结尾处表达了对母亲的理解,这是一种很好的情感升华。

这篇作文使用了高级句型。例如:使用 there be 句型,"There were so many wonderful moments that I've shared with my family and friends" 这句话使用 there be 句型来表达作者与家人和朋友共同分享美好时刻;使用时间状语从句,"When I was around five years old, I used to love playing with my sister's toys." 这句话使用了时间状语从句来描述作者在某一特定时期的行为和喜好。

总之,这篇文章情感真挚、叙事流畅,值得学习的地方包括生动的描绘、恰当的词句以及情感的升华,高级句型的使用也为文章增色不少。由此可知,隐性分层教学法的应用能有效帮助学生提高英语写作水平,同时也可以激发学生的学习兴趣和信心,让他们更加积极地参与到英语写作中来。

再举一例说明隐性分层教学法的有效性。小陈,一个八年级的学生,在英语写作中一直存在困扰。她总是担心自己的英语表达能力不够,尤其是在写议论文时。在隐性分层教学法的应用中,她被分到了提高层。老师为她设定了适合她的写作目标,并教给她一些关于议论文写作的基础知识。在开始写作前,老师按照提高层的写作要求,确定了议论文写作要达到的 6 个目标,并一一做了隐性指导:①文章论点清晰明确,有足够的说服力;②针对不同的观点或现象进行客观的分析,并能自圆其说;③使用具体的实例或数据支持自己的观点,增强说服力;④写作过程中注意逻辑性和连贯性,确保文章结构清晰、条理分明;⑤语言表达准确、流畅,语法和拼写错误较少;⑥文章结尾部分应总结全文,深化主题,并给出结论或建议。此外,老师鼓励小陈多与同伴进行讨论和交流。小陈学会了如何组织论点和论据以及如何使用恰当的词句来表达自己的观点。她还学会了如何"阅读"和理解别人的观点,并在自己的文章中予以回应。通过不断的练习和老师的反馈,她的写作水平逐渐提高,所用语法和词汇的准确率也得以提升。除此之外,她还积极参与小组讨论和交流,与其他学生一起学习和分享经验。她发现,与同伴的交流不仅有助于她更好地理解议论文的写作要求,还能激发她的写作灵感。最终,她在议论文写作方面取得很大进步,成为同学和老师眼中的"明星",她的很多议论文作品被老师选为佳作,在同学之间传阅研习。下面呈现小陈在接受隐性分层教学法前后针对"学生是否应该带手机到学校"这一话题的议论文作品,两相对比后就可以看出隐性分层教学法起到的实际作用。

小陈接受隐性分层教学之前的文章(含有一定错误,仅做展示之用):

Whether Students Should Bring Their Mobile Phones to School or Not?

Should students bring their mobile phones to school or not? In my opinion, it depends. If we use them properly, mobile phones can help improve learning efficiency and add the communication between students and teachers. However, if misused, they may have a big and bad impact on learning and teaching. Therefore, I think that it is necessary to set appropriate policies and guidelines to balance the use of mobile phones in and out of class.

上述短文给读者的最明显的感受就是无话可说,仅凭三言两语就片面、直接地回答了一个问题,给出了论点,但论据不够充分,用词不够精准,例如:"加强师生沟通"的短语中使用 add,不符合语言逻辑,使用 promote 更为恰当;a big and bad impact 中 bad 一词的选用使观点显得过于绝对,如果改用 negative 则较为妥帖。

小陈接受隐性分层教学之后的文章:

Whether Students Should Bring Their Mobile Phones to School or Not?

When it comes to whether students should bring their mobile phones to school, it's a hotly debated topic among parents, teachers and students. On one hand, some people think that it's a convenient way to access resources and communicate with friends. On the other hand, others worry that it may distract students from their studies and cause addiction problems.

My opinion is that students should bring their mobile phones to school, but only under certain conditions. Firstly, it's important to establish clear rules about mobile phone use. Students should be reminded that mobile phones are only for academic purposes, such as checking homework or accessing educational websites. Secondly, schools should provide resources for students to study without the use of their mobile phones. For example, schools could provide laptops or computers for students to access online resources.

Another factor to consider is that students are growing up in a digital age and it's inevitable that they will use mobile phones. Therefore, it's better to have a positive approach to mobile phone use rather than prohibit it completely. For example, schools could provide a designated space for students to use their mobile phones for communication and entertainment purposes.

In conclusion, students should bring their mobile phones to school, but under strict conditions. It's essential to establish clear rules and resources to balance academic use and digital use. In addition, schools should also provide positive environments for mobile phone use, so that students can use their devices in a safe and constructive way.

在"教—学—评"环节,同学们从文章亮点、写作思路、表达观点的词句等方面与小陈同学交流。大家一致认为,本文的亮点在于作者通过清晰的逻辑和有条理的论述,表达了对学生是否应该带手机到学校这一问题的看法。作者认为学生应该带手机到学校,但学校需要建立明确的手机使用规则,并为学生提供其他学习资源以平衡手机的使用。同时,作者也强调了学校应该为学生提供积极的手机使用环境,以使学生在安全和建设性的方式下使用设备。在阐述自己的观点时,作者小陈在论述中使用了客观事实,如手机的普及、学生正处于数字时代等,来支持自己的观点,同时借助明确的逻辑顺序和段落区分来表达自己的观点,使读者可以轻松地理解作者的意图。学生可以从本文中学习到如何在现代社会中平衡学习与娱乐的相关信息,还可以了解学校应当如何管理学生的手机使用情况以确保他们在安全和建设性的环境中使用手机。对于这篇作文,老师给予了如下评价:

小陈同学的议论文写作值得肯定,文中表达观点的句子较多:

①...it's a hotly debated topic among parents, teachers and students. (……在父母、老师和学生中,这是一个争论激烈的话题。)

②On one hand, some people think... On the other hand, others worry...(一方面,有人认为……另一方面,有人担心……)

③My opinion is that...(我的观点是……)

④Firstly, it's important to establish clear rules about mobile phone use. (首先,重要的是建立关于手机使用的明确规则。)

⑤Secondly, schools should provide resources for students to study without the use of their mobile phones. (其次,学校应该提供资源,让学生不使用手机学习。)

⑥Another factor to consider is that...(需要考虑的另一个因素是……)

⑦... it's better to have a positive approach to mobile phone use rather than prohibit it completely. (……对于手机使用,采取积极的办法而不是完全禁止,是更好的。)

⑧In conclusion, ...(总之,……)

⑨It's essential to establish clear rules and resources to balance academic use and digital use. (为了平衡学术使用和数字使用,建立明确的规则和资源是至关重要的。)

⑩...schools should also provide positive environments for mobile phone use, so that students can use their devices in a safe and constructive way. (……学校还应该提供积极的手机使用环境,这样学生才能安全和建设性地使用他们的设备。)

文中过渡词使用恰当,能够使句子的逻辑更清晰,便于读者理解作者的观点。本文还具有清晰的逻辑结构,能够考虑多种观点,使文章更具有客观性和全面性。

接下来是另一个学生的示例。小王同学经过七、八年级的隐性分层训练,在九年级说明文写作中取得了显著的进步。他之前在英语写作方面一直深受困扰,尤其是说明文写作。但是,在接受了隐性分层教学法的英语教学之后,他逐渐找到了适合自己的学习方法和节奏。老师对他的英语水平进行了分层,为他提供了个性化的指导和支持,包括词汇拓展、语法纠正、写作技巧训练和范文分析等。针对词汇量有限的问题,老师提供了一些适合用于说明文的词汇和短语,帮助他拓展词汇量,为写作打下良好基础;针对语法错误较多的问题,老师给予他及时的纠正和指导,帮助他掌握正确的语法规则,提高写作质量;针对写作技巧不熟练的问题,老师帮助他选择合适的说明方法以及文章结构的组织方式等。在进行了前期的准备工作后,老师再用范文分析法,给他提供了一些优秀的说明文范文,让他分析范文的结构、语言和表达方式,帮助他学习和借鉴优秀范文的写作技巧。通过不断的练习和反思,小王同学逐渐掌握了说明文的写作技巧,能够准确使用词汇和语法结构,合理组织段落与篇章。他的作文开始得到老师的表扬和同学们的赞赏,他也逐渐对英语写作产生了浓厚的兴趣。最终,他在初中学业水平考试中取得了优异的成绩,英语说明文写作成为他的强项之一。这个例子表明,在初中英语写作教学中,隐性分层教学法能够有效地帮助不同层次的学生取得成功。下面是小王同学在接受隐性分层教学之前的自由写作(含有一定错误,仅做展示之用):

### My Life in School in Ninth Grade

My life in school in ninth grade was full of challenges and exciting moments. At first, I found it hard to fit the new environment and the pace of the curriculum, but with the help of my teachers and friends, I am gradually used to it.

In class, I often found myself lost in the teacher's lecture, but I tried my best to pay attention and make notes. Besides, I joined many after-school activities, such as sports and music, because they helped me relax and improve my personal skills.

On weekends, I usually took time with my family and friends, find new places and doing fun things together. However, I also found time to study and review, making sure to keep up with my studies.

Overall, my ninth grade experience was challenging but rewarding. I learned a lot about myself and grew as a person. Although there were times when I felt overwhelmed, I never gave up and kept pushing forward. I am proud of what I have achieved and look forward to what the future holds.

作为一个经受两年英语写作训练的初中生,在接受隐性分层教学之前,小王同学的自由写作也表现得不错。语言、结构、语法等方面的错误较少,只是对自己的九年级学校生活的说明还是"轻描淡写",说明小王同学的写作深度和广度还是不够。实施隐性分层教学之后,老师专注在深度和广度方面给予他个性化指导,将他看作发展层学生,进行规范技巧性点拨,指出他在自由写作中存在的问题并加以改正。下面是小王同学接受隐性分层教学后的同主题作文:

My Life in School in Ninth Grade

My life in school in ninth grade is filled with challenges, opportunities, and experiences that shape me into the person I am today. Every morning, I wake up early and prepare myself for the day ahead. At school, I get engaged in various classes including maths, English, science, history, and even social studies. I particularly enjoy my English class because it provides me with an opportunity to expand my vocabulary and improve my writing skills. In addition to academics, I also participate in physical education and music class, which not only keep me physically fit but also help me develop an appreciation for different forms of music.

Apart from classes, my school offers various clubs and activities that allow me to explore my interests and hone my skills. I join in the school's debate club, where I am able to practice my speaking skills through participation in debates. Additionally, I participate in the school's basketball team, in which I not only develop my physical abilities but also make new friends. Socializing is an important aspect of my school life. I interact with my classmates and teachers on a daily basis, and we share our experiences and perspectives. Through these interactions, I have made friends that have helped me cope with challenges and become a more well-rounded person.

Overall, my life in school in ninth grade is a fulfilling experience that has allowed me to grow both academically and personally. I have learned valuable lessons that have shaped me into the person I am today, and I am excited about the opportunities that await me in the coming years.

In the future, I hope to continue to push myself academically and explore new interests. I also plan to continue participating in clubs and activities that help me develop my skills and make new friends. Through continued exploration and effort, I believe that I can achieve my goals and become a better person.

在英语课堂上，老师带领学生对这篇作文进行评价。学生的评价结果可总结为以下几个方面：

①文章内容丰富，表达清晰。文章涵盖了作者的九年级学校生活的各个方面，包括学术、体育、音乐、社交等，让读者对作者的九年级学校生活有全面的了解。②表达情感真挚。作者对学校生活的热爱和感激之情贯穿全文，让读者感受到作者对学校生活的珍视和投入。③文章语言流畅，用词准确。作者使用了许多生动的词汇和表达方式，使文章生动有趣。④文章结构合理，逻辑严谨。作者在文章中不仅描述了九年级学校生活的各个方面，还交代了在各个方面的收获。作者有过的挑战和机遇塑造了今天的自己：作者在学校中参加的各种课程、俱乐部和活动帮助他探索自己的兴趣爱好和技能，作者在学校中的社交互动帮助他交到朋友、应对挑战并成为更全面的人。因此，作者对未来充满期待，计划继续努力探索新兴趣、继续参加俱乐部和活动并实现自己的目标。

在学生对小王同学的作文做出评价后，老师也给出了自己的评价：

这篇文章展示了一个九年级学生对学校生活的全面认识和积极态度。文章内容丰富、表达清晰、情感真挚、语言流畅，使用了很多生动的词汇和表达方式，作文质量很好，可见隐性分层教学法在写作教学和写作学习中起到很大作用。本文的亮点在于作者借助定语从句描述了自己参加各种课程、俱乐部和活动以及与同学和老师进行社交互动后的收获。作者对定语从句的灵活和完美运用，充分说明了隐性分层教学法中个性化指导的成功。同时，作者对未来的积极展望和计划也展现了成长和进步。这篇文章应当收获很高的评价，以鼓励学生在学校生活中继续积极参与、勇于探索，实现个人更大的发展。

# 第二章 教学实践

本章主要介绍隐性分层教学法在初中英语写作教学中的具体应用。义务教育教科书初中阶段的英语教材(人民教育出版社 2013 年版,以下简称"人教版教材")共 5 本,英语写作体裁涵盖记叙文、应用文、说明文、议论文等各种文体。教师在处理这些写作教学任务时,有时会感到力不从心。在隐性分层教学法应用于教学实践时,笔者设置了两种写作实践模式。第一种要求基础层仿写句子、提高层扩写句子、发展层连句成章。随着年级的上升,笔者又增加了"师生互动:修辞润色"环节,以方便各层级学生相互学习和借鉴。第二种是情景设置,也就是在短文中设置空格,要求不同层级的学生完成不同的任务:基础层学生要根据语境,用所给词或短语的正确形式填空,使句意通顺;提高层学生要根据括号内所给信息填空;发展层学生的任务难度相对较大,需要根据指令完成任务或补全作文。

人教版教材各单元的写作内容主要包括单元主题写作、功能性写作、描述性写作、记叙性写作、读写结合。单元主题写作是人教版教材根据单元主题设计相应的写作任务,旨在帮助学生运用所学的语言知识和技能来表达自己的观点和感受。功能性写作是人教版教材为培养学生的实际应用能力,需要学生完成写电子邮件、请假条、邀请函等实用性较强的写作任务。描述性写作是人教版教材通过描写人物、事件、物品等,培养学生的描述能力和表达能力,使学生能够用英语准确、生动地表达自己的想法。记叙性写作是人教版教材为培养学生的叙事能力,通过设计相应的写作任务,帮助学生学会用英语叙述故事、描述经历等。读写结合是人教版教材将阅读与写作相结合,通过阅读材料的学习,帮助学生积累语言知识、拓展写作思维,为写作任务积累素材和思路。此外,人教版教材还根据不同年级和单元的特点,设计了有针对性的写作任务和评价标准,旨在培养学生的写作兴趣、自信心和语言运用能力。现根据人教版教材,给出隐性分层教学法在每个单元的写作教学中的具体应用。

## 第一节 七年级上册

七年级上学期,考虑到学生刚开始进入初中阶段的学习,教师在写作教学中主要采用汉译英的引导模式,要求基础层仿写简单句、提高层扩写简单句、发展层将简单句连成一篇短小的文章。七年级下学期,学生有了一定的单词、短语、句式、语法积累,也打下了一定的写作基础,教师延续七年级上学期的实践模式,让学生已培养起来的写作习惯和写作技巧得到巩固。

### Unit 1 My name's Gina.

#### ☞ 话题分析

本单元的写作话题是"介绍自己及物品"。学生在写作时,要介绍自己和他人的汉语名字、英语名字、电话信息、住址等,尽量使用礼貌用语。介绍自己时一般用第一人称,介绍物品时一般用第三人称。时态以一般现在时为主。

#### ☞ 素材积累

【单词】

middle 中间的　school 学校　hobby 爱好

【短语】

phone/telephone number 电话号码

last name 姓氏

first name 名字

ID number 身份证号

in the middle (of sth.) 在(……的)中央

middle school 中学

【句型】

What is her name? 她的名字是什么?

What's her telephone number? 她的电话号码是多少?

## ☞ 典例剖析

> 假如你是李华,刚升入初中,请向你的新同学介绍自己以及你书包里的三件物品。
>
> 要求:1. 包含以上所有信息,60 个词以上。
>
> 2. 用词恰当,语句连贯,使用连接词至少两次。
>
> 3. 句型丰富多样,包括疑问句和陈述句。
>
> 4. 不得出现真实的姓名和学校名。

**第一步:读题审题**

审
- 主题:介绍自己或物品
- 体裁:记叙文
- 时态:一般现在时
- 人称:第一人称;第三人称

**第二步:写作提纲**

姓名:My first name is ________(名), and my last name is ________.

年龄:I'm ________ years old./I'm a ________-year-old boy/girl.

电话:My phone number is ________.

班级:I'm in Class ________, Grade ________.

学校:I'm in ________ Middle School.

国籍:I'm from ________./I'm a Chinese/English/American...boy/girl.

爱好:I like ________(v.-ing)/. My favorite is ________./I enjoy ________(v.-ing).

第三步:分层写作

基础层:仿写句子

This is... 这是……

【例句】这是我的好朋友,她是 Mary Brown。

This is my good friend. She is Mary Brown.

【仿写】这是我的同学,他是 Jack。

This is my classmate, Jack.

Her/His telephone number is... 她的/他的电话号码是……

【例句】她的电话号码是 302-9617.

Her telephone number is 302-9617.

【仿写】我的电话号码是 0931-8659926.

My telephone number is 0931-8659926.

提高层:扩写句子

This is my good friend. She is Mary Brown. Her first name(她的名字)is Mary. Her last name(她姓) is Brown. Her telephone number is 302-9617(她的电话是 302-9617).

发展层:连句成章

Hi, everyone! I'm Li Hua. Hua is my first name and Li is my last name. I'm 13 years old. My phone number is 714-6962. I'm a Chinese boy. Now, I'm a student in Class Two, Grade Seven, No. 1 Middle School. I like reading books with my friends in the afternoon.

Look! This is my schoolbag. I have some school things in it. This is my ruler. It's a nice ruler. What color is it? It's blue and white. And what's that? It's a pen. The pen is red. Oh, those are my notebooks. I like black best, so they're black.

How about you? What's in your schoolbag?

## Unit 2  This is my sister.

### ☞ 话题分析

本单元的中心话题是“介绍他人”,要求学生在完成第一单元自我介绍的基础上,学会介绍人物和辨别人物。学生要在阅读相关人物简介的基础上,能运用指示代词独立完成简单的人物介绍。

### ☞ 素材积累

【单词】

grandfather 爷爷/姥爷　father 父亲　grandmother 奶奶/姥姥　mother 妈妈　friend 朋友　aunt 姑姑　picture 照片　son 儿子

【短语】

two photos of my family 我家庭的两张照片

in the first/next photo 在第一张/下一张照片中

the name of the dog 狗的名字

a family photo 一张家庭照/全家福

【句型】

Hi. I'm.../My name is... 你好。我是……/我的名字是……

Here is a photo of my family. 这有一张我家人的照片。

This is my... 这是我的……

These are my...and... 这些是我的……和……

### ☞ 典例剖析

假如你是 Lucy,你给家里人拍了一张全家福,照片里有爷爷奶奶、爸爸妈妈、姑姑 Lucy 和叔叔 Tom、哥哥 Tony 和 Jim,以及你自己。请你根据以上介绍写一段话,在英语课上给同学们讲一讲你的家庭。

**第一步:读题审题**

审
- 主题:介绍自己或者家人
- 体裁:记叙文
- 时态:一般现在时
- 人称:介绍自己时用第一人称;介绍他人时用第三人称

**第二步:写作提纲**

| 行文 | 构思 | 提纲 |
|---|---|---|
| 开头 | 简单介绍自己,引出自己拍的全家福 | My name is…<br>Here is a photo of… |
| 过程 | 具体介绍家庭成员 | This is… That is…<br>These are… Those are…<br>Who's she/he? She/He is…<br>Her/His name is… |
| 结尾 | 抒发对家庭的情感 | I have a happy family. /I love my family! |

**第三步:分层写作**

*基础层:仿写句子*

a photo of/photos of ……的照片

【例句】这些是 Mary Brown 的照片。

Here are photos of Mary Brown.

【仿写】这是我们家的几张照片。

Here are several photos of my family.

a happy family 一个幸福的家庭

【例句】杰克有一个幸福的家庭。

Jack has a happy family.

【仿写】我有一个幸福的五口之家。

I have a happy family of five.

提高层:扩写句子

【例句】These are…(扩写“我的爷爷奶奶”)

→These are my grandparents.

【练习】… my uncle Tom, and my aunt Lucy. (扩写“他们是”)

→They are my uncle Tom, and my aunt Lucy.

发展层:连句成章

Hi, I'm Lucy. Here is a photo of my family. These are my grandparents and my parents. They are very nice. Who are next to my parents? They are my aunt Lucy and my uncle Tom. These boys are my brothers, Tony and Jim. Who's the girl in the middle of the photo? It's me! I love my family.

## Unit 3 Is this your pencil?

### ☞ 话题分析

本单元以“教室里的物品”为话题,相关的写作要求是学生能用英语写出寻物启事或失物招领。这两种均属于应用文体裁,要求语言简练、表达明确。写寻物启事要紧扣主题,写清物品名称、联系人及联系方式,做到表述明确、语言简洁。写失物招领需要直接介绍捡到的物品(what),描述物品特征、捡到的时间和地点等。

### ☞ 素材积累

【单词】

found 找到;发现(find 的过去式) lost 失去(lose 的过去式) pencil 铅笔 pen 钢笔 eraser 橡皮 schoolbag 书包 dictionary 字典 notebook 笔记本 baseball 棒球

【短语】

a set of keys 一串钥匙

in the school library 在学校图书馆里

in the classroom 在教室里

ask sb. for sth. 向某人索要某物

call sb. at…给某人打电话

e-mail sb. at 给某人发邮件

**【句型】**

开头句：

①Found：I found a set of keys.

②Lost：I lost a dictionary.

③I found a blue pencil box in the school library today.

④I lost my schoolbag in the school library on Monday morning.

中间句：

①The pencil box is…

②A green pen, two white erasers and a yellow ruler are in it.

③Is this your…?

④Are these keys/books…yours?

⑤I must find it.

结尾句：

①Please call me at…

②You can e-mail me at…

③Thank you for your help.

## ☞ 典例剖析

### 失物招领

假如你是 David，你今天在学校图书馆里捡到一个蓝色的铅笔盒，里面有一支绿色的钢笔、两块白色的橡皮和一把黄色的尺子。请你写一则失物招领启事，张贴在学校的公告栏里。你的电话号码是 359-4781，你的电子邮箱是 david365@ 126. com。

**第一步:读题审题**

审
- 主题:失物招领
- 体裁:应用文
- 人称:第一人称;第三人称
- 时态:一般现在时

**第二步:写作提纲**

开篇点题(确定标题类型):Found

介绍物品(详细描述捡到的物品的特征,如颜色、数量等):a green pen, two white erasers and a yellow ruler

联系方式(注明联系方式):You can call me at.../You can e-mail me at...

**第三步:分层写作**

基础层:仿写句子

call sb. at ... 给某人打电话

【例句】请拨打李先生电话 0931-8512356。
Please call Mr. Li at 0931-8512356.

【仿写】请拨打我们办公室电话 0931-6685367。
Please call our office at 0931-6685367.

Ask...for... 向……咨询或索要……

【例句】向老师索要它。Ask the teacher for it.

【仿写】向妈妈要点钱。
Ask mom for some money.

提高层:扩写句子

【例句】I found the keys. (扩写地点"在图书馆")
→I found the keys in the library.

【练习】E-mail me. (扩写邮箱地址"Mary@ 163. com")
→E-mail me at Mary@ 163. com.

发展层:连句成章

Found

I found a blue pencil box in the school library today. A green pen, two white erasers and a yellow ruler are in it. Is it yours? My phone number is 359-4781. You can e-mail me at david365@ 126. com, too.

**寻物启事**

Helen 不小心弄丢了自己的书包,她必须找到这个书包。请你根据下面表格中的信息,以 Helen 的名义写一则寻物启事,张贴在学校门口的布告栏里。

| 姓名 | Helen |
|---|---|
| 遗失的物品 | 书包(书包是紫色的,里面有一本英语词典、一块红色的手表、一串钥匙、一些书和一个铅笔盒) |
| 时间 | 星期一早晨 |
| 地点 | 学校图书馆 |
| 联系方式 | 电话号码:568-3689　　邮箱地址:Helen888@ 126. com |

**第一步:读题审题**

审
- 主题:寻物启事
- 体裁:应用文
- 人称:第一人称;第三人称
- 时态:一般现在时

**第二步:写作提纲**

开篇点题(确定标题类型):Lost

介绍物品(详细描述捡到的物品的特征,如颜色、数量等):It's purple. An English dictionary, a red watch, a set of keys, some books and a pencil box are in it.

联系方式(注明联系方式):You can call me at .../You can e-mail me at ...

**第三步:分层写作**

基础层:仿写句子

lose sth. spl. 把某物落在某地

【例句】我把钢笔落在教室里了。I lost my pen in the classroom.

【仿写】我把钥匙落在书桌里了。I lost my keys in my desk.

提高层:扩写句子

I lost my schoolbag.(扩写时间状语“周一早晨”、地点状语“学校图书馆”)

→ I lost my schoolbag <u>in the school library on Monday morning.</u>

发展层:连句成章

Lost

I lost my schoolbag in the school library on Monday morning. It's purple. An English dictionary, a red watch, a set of keys, some books and a pencil box are in it. I must find it. Please call me at 568-3689 or you can e-mail me at Helen888@126. com.

Thank you for your help.

Helen

## Unit 4 Where's my schoolbag?

### ☞ 话题分析

本单元的话题是“房间里的物品”,要求学生能用英语描述某空间内一些物品的位置关系。此类作文属于说明文体裁,要求语言准确、有条理。时态常用一般现在时,人称常用第一、三人称。写作思路分三步:

第一步:确定介绍的对象,如“我的房间/我家的客厅”等;

第二步:运用方位介词来描述物品的位置;

第三步:对描述对象的感受及其他拓展性语言。

### ☞ 素材积累

【单词】

tidy 干净、整洁 clock 闹钟 desk 桌子 chair 椅子 bookcase 书柜 player 播放机

【短语】

in my room 在我的房间里

in the bookcase 在书柜里

on my desk 在我的桌子上

next to 紧邻

under the chair 在椅子下面

tape player 磁带播放器

**【句型】**

This is my room. 这是我的房间。It's nice and tidy. 它是干净、整洁的。

Where is my room? 我的房间在哪？I love my room. 我爱我的房间。

There is a desk in my room. 在我的房间里有一张桌子。

The+物品+be(is/are)+介词短语. 某物在某个位置。

## ☞ 典例剖析

请根据以下提示，以"My Room"为题，用英语写一篇短文，向你的朋友介绍一下你的房间。40 个词左右。

提示：

①既大又整洁；

②书桌上：一支钢笔、一个书包、五本书；

③墙上：一张地图、一张全家福；

④椅子下面：一个篮球。

**第一步：读题审题**

审：
- 主题：介绍房间
- 体裁：说明文
- 人称：第一人称；第三人称
- 时态：一般现在时

**第二步：写作提纲**

段落布局：
- 引出话题：Hello, everyone! This is my room.
- 物品位置：There is(are) ________ in my room. I have ________ in my room. In my room, you can see ________.
- 表达感受：I love my room very much!

**第三步:分层写作**

基础层:仿写句子

This is... 这是……

【例句】这是我的房间,干净整洁。

This is my room, clean and tidy.

【仿写】这是我妹的房间,乱七八糟。书本到处都是。

This is my sister's room, untidy. Books are everywhere.

a picture of... ……的照片

【例句】我的一张照片在墙上。

A picture of me is on the wall.

【仿写】我的全家福在桌子上。

A picture of my family is on the desk.

提高层:扩写句子

【例句】Is there a computer?(扩写放电脑的地点"在卧室")

→Is there a computer in the bedroom?

【练习】My room is not tidy, but...(扩写自己的观点"我非常喜欢它")

→My room is not tidy, but I like it very much.

发展层:连句成章

My Room

Hi, everyone! This is my room. It is big and tidy. There are many things in it. Well, you can see the table. A pen, a schoolbag and five books are on it. On the wall, there is a map and a family photo. Under my chair is a basketball. I like my room. What about you?

## Unit 5 Do you have a soccer ball?

### ☞ 话题分析

本单元的话题是"与朋友共度快乐时光",要求学生能用英语谈论体育用品及体育活动。学生需要介绍自己或他人对体育用品的收藏和进行体育锻炼的情况,并简单阐述自己对某项运动的观点;学生也可以介绍自己喜欢或不喜欢的体育运动,并说明理由。

## ☞ 素材积累

【单词】

球类:basketball 篮球　volleyball 排球　soccer ball 足球　badminton 羽毛球　ping-pong ball 乒乓球

【短语】

play basketball/volleyball/baseball 打篮球/排球/棒球

play soccer 踢足球

play sports 做运动

watch TV 看电视

on TV 在电视上;通过电视

after class 课后

after school 放学后

【句型】

I love playing sports. 我喜爱做运动。

I think... is very interesting/boring. 我认为……非常有趣/无聊。

It is easy/difficult... for me...我认为……对我来说是简单的/困难的……

I only watch it on TV. 我只在电视上观看它/我只通过电视观看它。

Sports are good for us. 运动对我们有好处。

## ☞ 典例剖析

假如你是李华,是一个爱运动的男孩。请你以"I Like Sports"为题,写一篇 60 个词左右的短文。

**第一步:读题审题**

审
- 主题:运动
- 体裁:说明文
- 时态:一般现在时
- 人称:第一人称

**第二步:写作提纲**

第一段(主题句):I like sports very much…

第二段(正文句):what, how many, when, who, why…

第三段(结尾句):Sports are good for us…

**第三步:分层写作**

*基础层:仿写句子*

I have… but I don't have… 我有……但是没有……

【例句】我有篮球但是没有足球。

I have a basketball but I don't have a soccer ball.

【仿写】我有三个足球,但是没有排球。

I have three soccer balls but I have no volleyball.

play sth. with sb. 与某人一起玩某物

【例句】我经常和我同桌一起踢足球。I often play soccer with my table mate.

【仿写】你能和我一起去兰州大学踢球吗?

Can you go to Lanzhou University to play football with me?

*提高层:扩写句子*

【例句】I think it is good for me.(扩写动词不定式"打篮球")

→I think it is good for me to play basketball.

【练习】Do you often watch games?(扩写方式"通过电视")

→ Do you often watch games on TV?

*发展层:连句成章*

### I Like Sports

Hello, my name is Li Hua. I like sports.

I have two basketballs and three soccer balls. I don't play volleyball. I think it is difficult for me. I only watch it on TV. I think soccer is easy and fun for me, so I often play it with my classmates after school. I don't have a baseball. I think it's boring.

Sports are good for us. What sports do you like? Please tell me.

## Unit 6 Do you like bananas?

### ☞ 话题分析

本单元以“食物”为话题，要求学生谈论对食物的喜恶。学生需要用“like句型”谈论对食物的喜恶和一日三餐的饮食习惯。学生可以使用“总—分—总”法写此类作文：第一个“总”指开篇点题，引出话题；“分”指分别介绍；第二个“总”指总结评价。时态常用一般现在时，人称用第一、三人称。

### ☞ 素材积累

【单词】

like 喜欢 eat 吃 breakfast 早餐 lunch 午餐 dinner 晚餐 healthy 健康 fat 肥胖 egg 鸡蛋 fruit 水果 salad 沙拉 vegetable 蔬菜 milk and bread 牛奶和面包 carrot 胡萝卜 hamburger 汉堡包 tomato 西红柿 banana 香蕉 apple 苹果 pear 梨 rice 米饭 strawberry 草莓 chicken 鸡肉

【短语】

think about 思考，思索

eating habit 饮食习惯

eat well 吃得好

for breakfast/lunch/dinner 作为早/午/晚餐

healthy food 健康的食物

【句型】

I have a… eating habit. 我有一个……的饮食习惯。

I like/don't like…我喜欢/不喜欢……

For breakfast/lunch/dinner, I eat/have…我吃……作为早餐/午餐/晚餐。

I don't want to be fat, so I don't eat/have…我不想变胖，所以我不吃……

I think… is/are healthy/unhealthy food. 我认为……是健康/不健康食品。

How/what about your eating habits? 你的饮食习惯是什么样的?

## ☞ 典例剖析

请你根据下表内容,写一篇小短文,谈一谈你一日三餐的饮食喜好。

| | |
|---|---|
| 早餐 | 牛奶、面包和一个鸡蛋 |
| 午餐 | 米饭、鸡肉和蔬菜 |
| 晚餐 | 沙拉和水果 |
| 其他 | 不想变胖,所以不吃汉堡包 |

**第一步:读题审题**

审:
- 体裁:说明文
- 主题:饮食爱好
- 人称:第一人称;第三人称
- 时态:一般现在时

**第二步:写作提纲**

第一段(描述饮食习惯):I have a healthy eating habit. I eat well every day.

第二段(介绍三餐饮食):For breakfast, I have… For lunch, I eat… For dinner, I like eating… I think… I don't want…

第三段(结尾发起疑问):How about…? Please tell me about them.

**第三步:分层写作**

基础层:仿写句子

For breakfast/lunch/dinner, sb. like… 早餐/午餐/晚餐,某人喜欢……

**【例句】**早餐,Linda 喜欢吃面包。

For breakfast, Linda likes to have bread.

**【仿写】**午餐,他喜欢汉堡和沙拉,但他不喜欢吃鸡肉。

For lunch, he likes hamburgers and salad, but he doesn't like chicken.

eating habit 饮食习惯

**【例句】**我们应该有一个良好的饮食习惯吗?

Should we have a good eating habit?

**【仿写】**你的饮食习惯怎么样?

How/What about your eating habits?

提高层：扩写句子

【例句】For dinner, I like chicken and rice.（扩写不喜欢的食物“鸡蛋”）

→For dinner, I like chicken and rice, but I don't like eggs.

【练习】I think…（扩写宾语从句）

→I think they are healthy.

发展层：连句成章

I have a healthy eating habit. I eat well every day. For breakfast, I have milk, bread and an egg. For lunch, I eat rice, chicken and vegetables. For dinner, I like eating salad and fruit. I think hamburgers are unhealthy food. I don't want to be fat, so I don't eat them. How about your eating habits? Please tell me about them.

## Unit 7 How much are these socks?

### ☞ 话题分析

本单元以“如何写一则广告”为话题。写作时，开篇进行宣传，多为号召性语言；然后介绍产品物美价廉，有各种样式可供选择，且针对不同人群有不同样式，达到激起顾客购买欲望的目的，细节要具体到品种、颜色、价位等；结尾要再次号召大家购买，做到首尾呼应。

### ☞ 素材积累

【单词】

服装类：store 商店 hat 帽子 bag 包 socks 袜子 skirt 衬衫 sweater 毛衣 color 颜色 pair 双/对

买卖类：sell 卖 price 价格 sale 销售

【短语】

at a good price 价格合理

clothes store 服装店

buy clothes 买衣服

for boys/girls 对男孩子/女孩子而言

skirt in red 红色的裙子

for only 15 dollars 只卖 15 美元

come to… 来……

【句型】

Come and buy…at our great sale. 来买吧,我们的……特价销售。

Do you have time…? 你有时间……吗?

Welcome to… 欢迎来……

We have a great sale. 我们有特价活动。

What you need is what we have! 你想要的,我们都有!

Come and buy what you need at our store now. 现在快来我们店里购买你想要的吧。

I'm in … clothes store. 我在……服装店。

## ☞ 典例剖析

> 假如你家附近的 Mary 服装店正在进行大减价促销活动,请你为其写一则广告,吸引顾客前来消费。
>
> 内容包括:1. 有哪些商品;2. 商品的价格、颜色等如何。
>
> 作文要求:1. 不能照抄原文;不得在作文中出现学校的真实名称和学生的真实姓名。2. 语句连贯,60 个词左右。

**第一步:读题审题**

审
- 主题:卖衣服广告
- 体裁:说明文
- 人称:第一人称
- 时态:一般现在时

**第二步:写作提纲**

段落布局
- 开头(吸引人的句子):点出商店名字(come and buy your clothes at Mary's Clothes Store)
- 正文(所给要点写全):所售商品及其价格、颜色等(we have+商品+in+颜色+for+价格)
- 结尾(宣传语):言简意赅(come to our store now)

第三步:分层写作

基础层:仿写句子

for only+价格　只卖……(价格)

【例句】我们的帽子只需 6.6 元。

We have hats for only 6.6 yuan.

【仿写】我们的裤子只需 15 美元。

We have trousers for only 15 dollars.

at very good prices/at great sale 以优惠价格

【例句】快来用优惠价格买你的衣服吧!

Come and buy your clothes at great sale!

【仿写】快来用优惠价格买你的鞋子吧!

Come and buy your shoes at great sale!

提高层:扩写句子

【例句】We sell skirt.(扩写所卖的价格“只卖 5 元”)

→We sell skirt for only 5 yuan.

【练习】How much is/are…?(扩写衣服种类“袜子”)

→ How much are these socks?

发展层:连句成章

Welcome to Mary's Clothes Store. Come and buy your clothes at good prices. We have a great sale in our store. We have clothes for men, women, boys and girls at very good prices.

We have jackets for men in yellow, blue, white and black for 150 yuan. We have nice hats for women in red and white for only 30 yuan. Do you need bags for sports? We have bags for sports for only 120 yuan. We have trousers in all kinds of colors for 70 yuan. And shorts are only 50 yuan. For girls, we have nice red skirts for only 50 yuan. Do you need socks? Socks are only 10 yuan for three pairs.

Come and buy clothes now! Don't miss it!

## Unit 8 When is your birthday?

### ☞ 话题分析

本单元的话题是“谈论日期”,主要是谈论生日、节日和一些其他活动的日期。在介绍生日或有关活动安排时,要正确使用基数词和序数词,注意日期的常用表达。

### ☞ 素材积累

【单词】

festival 节日　busy 忙碌的;无暇的　time 时间

【短语】

Children's Day 儿童节

Women's Day 妇女节

New Year's Day 新年

Mother's Day 母亲节

Father's Day 父亲节

Spring Festival 春节(农历新年)

Lantern Festival 元宵节

Tomb-Sweeping Day 清明节

Dragon Boat Festival 端午节

Mid-Autumn Festival 中秋节

Double Ninth Festival 重阳节

the Night of the Seventh Lunar Calendar Festival 七夕节

Chinese New Year's Eve 除夕

this term 这学期

next month 下个月

have an English party 举办一场英语晚会

have a book sale 举办一场图书促销会

have a good time (表示祝福)过得愉快

do one's homework 做某人的家庭作业

have a basketball game 举行一场篮球赛

want to do sth. 想要做某事

【句型】

Do you like/have…? 你喜欢/有……吗?

Please come to … next week/this Friday. 请下周/这周五来……(某地)。

We have a/an… It's on … 我们举行……(活动)。它在……(日期)。

On…, we have a/an… in… 在……(日期),我们在……(某地)举行……(活动)。

See you there! /Have a good time! 那里见! /祝你玩得高兴!

## ☞ 典例剖析

假如你是 Alice,请给你的朋友写一张便条,邀请他/她下周日上午参加你的十三岁生日聚会。

写作要点:①你的朋友是谁?②为什么邀请他/她来参加你的生日聚会?③什么时候举办生日聚会?④生日聚会上有什么活动?

要求:①语句通顺,意思连贯,语法正确,格式无误,书写规范;②文中不得出现真实的人名、校名或地名;③词数不少于60。

**第一步:读题审题**

审
- 主题:邀请他人
- 体裁:书信体记叙文
- 人称:第一人称
- 时态:一般现在时

**第二步:写作提纲**

段落布局
- 开头(询问):Do you want to…?
- 正文(活动):We have a/an…
- 结尾(委婉邀请):Please come to…

**第三步:分层写作**

基础层:仿写句子

come to my birthday party 来参加我的生日聚会

【例句】请本周末来参加我的生日聚会。

Please come to my birthday party on the weekend.

【仿写】你下周来参加我的生日聚会吗？

Would you come to my birthday party next week?

Have a good time! 玩得高兴!

【例句】祝你北京之行开心! Have a good time to Beijing!

【仿写】祝你新加坡之行开心!

Have a good time to Singapore!

提高层:扩写句子

【例句】It is on September.（扩写具体日期“28 日”）

→It is on September 28th.

【练习】We will have a soccer game.（扩写具体时间“下周三”）

→We will have a soccer game next Wednesday.

发展层:连句成章

Dear Helen,

My birthday is on June 5th, next Sunday. I will be 13 years old. I really hope you can come to my party, because you are my best friend. The birthday party is from 10:00 a. m. to 6:30 p. m.

At the party, we will eat a big birthday cake and some nice food. There are many interesting activities at the party. We can sing, dance and play some games. I am sure we will have a great time.

Yours,

Alice

## Unit 9　My favorite subject is science.

### ☞ 话题分析

本单元的话题是“学校功课安排”，要求学生能指出个人喜欢的学科并说明理由。学生需要能够准确运用类似 at 8:30、from 10:00 to 10:45、on Monday、on Friday afternoon 的短语来表述时间，以及能够结合语境准确使用 because、but、and、then、after that 等连接词。

## ☞ 素材积累

【单词】

学科名词：Chinese 语文　math 数学　English 英语　history 历史　geography 地理　science 科学　music 音乐　P. E. 体育　art 艺术

修饰学科的形容词：fun 有趣　difficult 困难　easy 容易　boring 无聊　useful 有用

星期：Monday 星期一　Tuesday 星期二　Wednesday 星期三　Thursday 星期四　Friday 星期五　Saturday 星期六　Sunday 星期日

【短语】

have math = have a math class 上数学课

have volleyball = play volleyball 打排球

be busy 忙碌的

be useful 有用的

be difficult 困难的

be interesting 有趣的

be boring 无聊的

be relaxing 放松的

be fun 有趣的

after lunch 午餐后

after class 下课后

for two hours 两个小时

【句型】

I want to meet you on Friday afternoon. 我想周五下午见你。

Is that OK with you? 那对你来说合适吗？

## ☞ 典例剖析

假如你是李华,请根据下面表格中的内容写一封电子邮件,把你星期五的活动情况告诉你的好朋友 Joe。

| Friday | | | |
|---|---|---|---|
| Time | Subject/Activity | Time | Subject/Activity |
| 8:00~8:50 | Chinese | 12:00~13:00 | Lunch |
| 9:00~9:50 | Math | 13:00~13:50 | Music |
| 10:00~10:50 | English | 14:00~14:50 | Geography |
| 11:00~11:50 | Art | 15:00~17:00 | Playing Basketball |

要求:1. 语句通顺、条理清楚; 2. 70 个词左右。

**第一步:读题审题**

审
- 主题:日常活动
- 体裁:记叙文
- 人称:第一人称
- 时态:一般现在时

**第二步:写作提纲**

段落布局
- 开头(自我介绍):I am really busy on ________.
- 正文(学科介绍和课外活动):At 8:00, I have ________.
- 结尾(总结感受,邀请互动):Please tell me about your school life.

**第三步:分层写作**

基础层:仿写句子

want to do sth. 想做某事

【例句】我想周六去拜访你。

I want to pay a visit to you on Saturday.

【仿写】你想喝点加蜂蜜的热茶吗?

Do you want to drink some hot tea with honey?

be OK with sb. 对某人来说是合适的

【例句】时间对琳达来说合适吗? Is the time OK with Linda?

【仿写】房间对玛丽来说可以吗?

Is the room OK with Mary?

提高层:扩写句子

【例句】I want to meet you on Friday afternoon. (扩写不能见面的转折语“但我真的很忙”)

→I want to meet you on Friday afternoon, but I am really busy.

【练习】It's fun. (扩写“上历史课”)

→It's fun to have history.

发展层:连句成章

Dear Joe,

I'm busy on Friday. At 8:00 I have Chinese. It's my favorite subject. Then I have math from 9:00 to 9:50. It's very difficult. After that I have English. It is fun. The last lesson in the morning is art. Lunch is from 12:00 to 13:00. I have music from 13:00 to 13:50. It's relaxing. And then I have geography. It's easy. After school, I play basketball with my classmates from 15:00 to 17:00.

How about you? What's your favorite subject?

Yours,

Li Hua

## 第二节 七年级下册

### Unit 1 Can you play the guitar?

#### ☞ 话题分析

本单元以“写招聘海报”为话题,要求学生写出一张招聘海报。学生在写作时应注意,招聘海报应该有醒目的标题,让人一眼就能明了招聘目的。招聘内容应分三个层次来写:①需要什么样的人员,即招聘职位;②说明招聘条件;③给出联系方式。体裁以应用文为主,时态多为一般现在时,人称多采用第二人称。

## ☞ 素材积累

【单词】

乐器:guitar 吉他　drum 鼓　piano 钢琴　violin 小提琴

俱乐部相关词汇:club 俱乐部;社团　join 参加;加入　swim 游泳(v./n.)　dance 跳舞(v.),舞蹈(n.)　draw 画　tell 讲述;告诉　write 写作;写字　music 音乐(→ musician 音乐家)

其他词汇:or 或者;也不(用于否定句)　make 使成为;制造　today 在今天　weekend 周末　teach 教,讲授(→ teacher n. 教师)

【短语】

play chess 下国际象棋

speak English 说英语

be good at… 擅长……

talk to… 跟……说

kung fu 功夫;武术

play the drums 敲鼓

be good with 善于处理……的;与……和睦相处

make friends 结交朋友

help (sb.) with sth. 在某方面帮助(某人)

the story telling club 讲故事俱乐部

English-speaking students 说英语的学生

on the weekend 在周末

【句型】

We hope that… 我希望……

Do you have time…? 你有……时间吗?

Are you free? 你有空吗?

One of the most important things is… 最重要的事情之一是……

If you… 如果你……

It's necessary for you to do sth. 你有必要做某事

## ☞ 典例剖析

尊敬老人是中华民族的传统美德。假设你是养老院(the old people's home)的负责人王强,在假期即将到来之际,你想要招聘与你志同道合、愿为公益事业服务的志愿者。请以此为话题拟一则招聘广告。30—50个词。

提示:1. 要求和老人相处和睦,能和老人下象棋……

2. 请有意者给你打电话,电话号码为686-7729。

**第一步:读题审题**

审
- 主题:招聘广告
- 体裁:应用文
- 人称:第二人称
- 时态:一般现在时

**第二步:写作提纲**

招聘职位:We need…; Do you want to…?

招聘条件:Are you good with…? Can you…? Are you good at…?

联系方式:Please call me at…

**第三步:分层写作**

基础层:仿写句子

need sb. 需要某人

【例句】我们需要养老院的志愿者。

We need volunteers at the old people's home.

【仿写】我们招聘暑假辅导老师。We need a teacher for summer holidays.

be good with 善于处理……的;与……和睦相处

【例句】你和孩子们相处和睦吗? Are you good with children?

【仿写】你和老人相处和睦吗? Are you good with the old?

提高层:扩写句子

【例句】Can you play chess? (扩写下棋对象"老人")

→Can you play chess with the old?

【练习】Are you good at…?（扩写“讲故事”）

→Are you good at telling stories?

发展层：连句成章

Volunteers Wanted

We need volunteers at the old people's home.

Do you want to help the old people? Are you good with the old? Can you play chess with the old? Are you good at telling stories?

Yes, then come and join us. Please call Wang Qiang at 686-7729.

## Unit 2 What time do you go to school?

### ☞ 话题分析

本单元以“谈论日常作息时间”为话题，要求学生学会熟练运用一般现在时，以及学会正确表达时间、正确使用频率副词来谈论自己的日常生活，合理安排自己的学习和课外活动时间。写作时通常使用第一人称和一般现在时。

### ☞ 素材积累

**【单词】**

morning 早晨　afternoon 下午　evening 傍晚　night 晚上

**【短语】**

get up 起床

go to school 上学

have lunch 吃午饭

take a break 休息

play sports 进行体育活动

do homework 做作业

go to bed 上床睡觉

busy but happy 忙碌但快乐

get dressed 穿衣服

## ☞ 典例剖析

根据表格中的内容,以"My Day"为题写一篇短文,按时间顺序写出自己一天的活动安排。70 个词左右。

| | |
|---|---|
| 起床 6:00 a. m. | 回家 5:00 p. m. |
| 吃早饭 6:30 a. m. | 吃晚饭 6:00 p. m. |
| 上学 7:40 a. m. | 做作业 7:20 p. m. |
| 上课 8:00 a. m. | 看电视 8:30 p. m. |
| 吃午饭 12:00 a. m. | 睡觉 9:30 p. m. |

**第一步:读题审题**

审
- 体裁:记叙文
- 人称:第一人称
- 时态:一般现在时

**第二步:写作提纲**

开头(beginning):I have a busy life/My daily life is busy.

正文(body):get up/go to school;have lunch;do homework…

结尾(ending):My life is busy, but I feel…/What a…life…!

**第三步:分层写作**

基础层:仿写句子

get up at…  ……起来

【例句】我每天六点起床。I get up at six every day.

【仿写】我们通常早晨 6:30 起床。<u>We usually get up at 6:30 a. m.</u>

start classes 上课

【例句】我的学校八点上课。My school starts classes at eight.

【仿写】我们学校九点开始上课。<u>Our school starts classes at nine.</u>

have a…life 过……生活

【例句】在中国我们过着愉快的生活。We have a happy life in China.

【仿写】我在学校过着忙碌的生活。<u>I have a busy life at school.</u>

提高层:扩写句子

【例句】I am busy.（扩写时间）

→I am busy every day/every night/now...

【练习】I do my homework.（扩写时间状语“吃完晚饭以后”）

→After eating dinner, I do my homework.

发展层:连句成章

My Day

Hi, friends! I want to tell you something about my day. I often get up at six o'clock in the morning. I have breakfast at half past six. I usually go to school at seven forty. My school starts at eight o'clock. I have lunch at twelve at school. I go home at five o'clock in the afternoon. Then I have dinner at about six o'clock. After dinner, I do my homework at seven twenty. I usually watch TV at half past eight and go to bed at half past nine.

I'm busy but happy.

## Unit 3 How do you get to school?

### ☞ 话题分析

本单元围绕“怎样到达目的地”话题,要求学生介绍自己或他人上学或上班的出行方式。学生首先要注意正确使用描述乘坐交通工具、两地距离和花费时间的短语和句型,然后表达自己对所提到的交通方式的评价。写作时要用一般现在时和第一人称。

### ☞ 素材积累

【单词】

train 火车 bus 公共汽车 subway 地铁 bike 自行车 car 小汽车;轿车 boat 小船

【短语】

**乘坐交通工具**

动词短语：

take the train 乘火车

take the bus 乘公共汽车

take the subway 乘地铁

ride a bike 骑自行车

take the boat 乘船

have/take a walk 散步

介词短语：

by train 乘火车

by subway 乘地铁

by bike 骑自行车

by boat 乘船

on foot 走路

**其他短语**

how far 多远

how long 多长时间

walk to school 步行去上学

get to school 到校

cross the river 过河

come true 实现;成为现实

【句型】

For many students, it is easy to get to school. 对于很多学生来说,上学是件很容易的事。

My school is about 20 kilometers from my home. 我的学校离我家大约 20 千米。

It takes about 40 minutes to get there by bus. 乘坐公共汽车去那儿大约要花费 40 分钟。

The bus ride is never boring because I always talk to my classmates. 公交车车

程并不无聊,因为我总是和我的同学聊天。

## ☞ 典例剖析

Tony 是湖畔中学(Lakeside Middle School)的一名中学生,他在班上做了一个关于同学们如何上学的一个调查。请根据以下提示,完成一篇作文:

1. 大多数同学走路去学校,因为他们的家离学校近。

2. 只有十个同学乘公交车去学校,他们很喜欢这样的方式,因为可以和同学聊天。

3. 有两个同学骑自行车上学,他们认为这样有利于身体健康。

4. Tony 的朋友 Alice 通常走路去学校,她的家离学校只有一千米,通常她走半个小时就能到。

要求:1. 内容包括提示中所有的写作要点;

2. 条理清楚,行文连贯,可适当发挥;

3. 文中不能出现真实的人名和地名等信息;

4. 词数不少于 80 个。

**第一步:读题审题**

审
- 体裁:应用文
- 时态:一般现在时
- 人称:第三人称

**第二步:写作提纲**

写出提示中的关键词句:

walk to school 步行到校

near school 在学校附近

take a bus 乘公交车

like the way 喜欢这种方式

talk with classmates 与同学们聊天

ride a bike to school 骑自行车上学

be good for…对……有好处

It is... kilometers/meters/miles from A to B 从A地到B地有……千米/米/英里。

It takes sb. some time to do sth. 某人花费多长时间去做某事。

**第三步:分层写作**

基础层:仿写句子

bus ride 公交车车程

【例句】公交车车程并不无聊,因为我总是和我的同学聊天。

The bus ride is never boring because I always talk to my classmates.

【仿写】公交车车程花费40分钟。The bus ride takes 40 minutes.

think of 思考;认为

【例句】Mary 想知道他怎样认为这个旅行。

Mary wants to know what he thinks of the trip.

【仿写】你怎样认为骑车去上学?

How do you think of going to school by bike?

提高层:扩写句子

【例句】For many students, it is easy to get to school.(扩写原因"因为有他们能使用的不同方式")

→For many students, it is easy to get to school because there are different ways they can use.

【练习】The bus ride is never boring.(扩写原因"因为我们能在车上相互交谈")

→The bus ride is never boring because we can talk with each other on the bus.

发展层:连句成章

Tony is a middle school student of Lakeside Middle School. He did a survey about the ways for his schoolmates to go to school. Most students walk to school, because their homes are near to school. Only ten students go to school by bus. They like the bus ride because they can talk with their classmates. Only two students ride bikes to school. They think it is good for health. Tony's friend Alice usually walks to school. Her home is only one kilometer from school. It usually takes her about half an hour to get to school from her home.

## Unit 4 Don't eat in class.

### ☞ 话题分析

本单元的中心话题为"介绍规则"。学生的作文中要包含所有提示内容,看法、观点等要恰当、合理。时态为一般现在时,注意 must、have to、can、can't 等词的恰当运用。写作时,常用书信形式呈现,同时应做好以下几点:

1. 根据题目要求先列提纲,所写规则要符合实际情况,内容要积极,看法要合理。

2. 选好能用到的句型、短语和单词等,如"I have to…"(我不得不……)、"I can…"(我能……)、"I can't…"(我不能……)等等。

3. 作文写好后要仔细检查,看单词拼写、所用句式、标点符号等是否正确,对于所给提示要点要做到不缺不漏。

### ☞ 素材积累

【单词】

过渡词:and 和;以及　but 但是　or 或者　then 然后　after… 在……之后

【短语】

家庭规则:

go out on school nights 上学日晚上外出

do homework after school 放学后做作业

do the dishes after dinner 晚餐后洗餐具

help one's mom make breakfast every morning 每天早上帮某人的妈妈做早餐

make one's bed 铺床

relax on weekends 周末放松

学校规则:

be late for class 上学迟到

be on time 准时

run in the hallways 在走廊跑步

be quiet in the library 在图书馆里保持安静

wear the school uniform 穿校服

keep one's hair short 留短发

【句型】

There are so many rules in my life. 我生活中有许多规则。

I have to/must/can/can't… 我不得不/必须/能/不能……

I never have fun/I never feel relaxed. What should I do? 我从来没快乐过/我从来没感觉放松过。我该怎么办?

We have many rules around us, but we should know: "No rules, no standards!" 我们周围有许多规则,但是我们应该知道:"没有规矩不成方圆。"

We must obey the rules, then we'll be safe and happy. 我们必须遵守规则,这样我们就会安全、快乐。

## ☞ 典例剖析

假如你是 Molly Brown,你的学校和家里的规矩很多,请你给 Dr. Know 写一封信,表达你的感受。

要求:1. 不少于 80 个词;

2. 语言规范,标点正确;

3. 符合书信格式。

**第一步:读题审题**

审
- 体裁:应用文
- 人称:第一人称
- 时态:一般现在时
- 动词:情态动词

**第二步:写作提纲**

第一段(main idea):Can you…? I…because there are…rules…

第二段(body):School rules and family rules… I must… and I must…;

I can't…or…; I can't…either.

第三段(your ideas):I never…

**第三步:分层写作**

基础层:仿写句子

too many rules 太多规矩

【例句】我家的规矩太多。There are too many rules in my home.

【仿写】我的学校有太多规矩。

There are too many rules in my school.

make one's bed 整理床铺

【例句】玛丽每晚不得不整理床铺。Mary has to make her bed every night.

【仿写】我小时候就学会自己整理床铺。

I learned to make my bed since I was a child.

提高层:扩写句子

【例句】I can't play basketball. (扩写时间状语"放学后")

→I can't play basketball after school.

【练习】My dad says I can't play basketball after school. (扩写条件"除非作业完成")

→My dad says I can't play basketball after school unless I finish my homework.

I run to school. (扩写原因"起床迟了")→I run to school because I get up late.

发展层:连句成章

Dear Dr. Know,

There are too many rules! At 6:00 a. m. , my mom says, "Get up now and make your bed!" After breakfast, my mom always says, "Don't leave the dirty dishes in the kitchen!"

After that, I run to school because I can't be late. At school, we have more rules — don't be noisy, don't eat in class. My dad says I can't play basketball after school because I must do my homework. I can play only on weekends. After dinner,

I can't relax either. I must read a book before I can watch TV. But I have to go to bed before 10:00 p. m. Rules, rules, rules! They're terrible! What can I do, Dr. Know?

Yours,

Molly Brown

## Unit 5 Why do you like pandas?

### ☞ 话题分析

本单元的话题是“谈论喜好”,内容围绕“动物”这一主题展开,学生通过了解各种动物,能够掌握表达对不同动物的喜好的能力,自身的写作技巧和方法也能得以完善。写以“动物”为话题的短文首先需要掌握描写动物时常用的词语,如 cute、clever、lovely、tall、lazy、interesting、small、big、friendly、shy、scary、beautiful、ugly 等,并应该对自己所描写的动物有一定程度的了解,明确自己写作的中心思想。学生在提高自身语言运用能力的同时,也能够提高自己热爱动物、热爱大自然的意识,进而培养对动物和自然的保护意识。

### ☞ 素材积累

【单词】

动物:elephant 大象 koala 考拉 panda 熊猫 giraffe 长颈鹿

可用于修饰动物的形容词:friendly 友好的 clever 机灵的 cute 可爱的 lazy 懒惰的 fun 有趣的 ugly 丑陋的

地名:Africa 非洲 South Africa 南非 Thailand 泰国 South/North America 南/北/美洲

【短语】

my favorite animal(s) 我最喜欢的动物(们)

cut down trees 砍树

save the elephants 拯救大象

be made of/from sth. 由……制成(of 后接看得见的原材料,from 后接看不

见的原材料）

get lost = lose one's way 迷路

help them（to）live 帮助他/她/它们居住

be friendly to us 对我们友好

（be）in big/great danger 陷入巨大的危险之中；（be）out of danger 脱离危险

a symbol of good luck 好运的象征

【句型】

What is your favorite animal？你最喜欢哪种动物？

What are your favorite animals？你最喜欢哪些动物？

Let's see the pandas first. 让我们先去看熊猫吧。

I like giraffes because they are kind of interesting and cute. 我喜欢长颈鹿，因为它们有点儿有趣且可爱。

## ☞ 典例剖析

请你根据中文要点提示，用英文写一段文字，简要介绍一下中国的国宝（national treasure）大熊猫（giant panda）。

产地：中国四川、陕西、甘肃等省份（province）。

体貌特征：黑白相间的毛皮（black and white fur），大眼睛，圆耳朵，身体虽胖但动作敏捷（move nimbly），非常招人喜爱。

喜好：最爱吃竹子（bamboo），会爬树、游泳。

寿命：一般为 18—30 年。

数量：很少，我们必须尽力保护（protect）好它们。

要求：1. 内容包括提示中所有的写作要点；

2. 条理清楚，行文连贯，可适当发挥；

3. 文中不能出现真实的人名和地名等信息；

4. 词数不少于 70 个。

首句已给出，不计入总词数。

Giant pandas are China's national treasure. ________________

**第一步:读题审题**

审{
主题:动物(大熊猫)
体裁:记叙文
人称:第三人称
时态:一般现在时

**第二步:写作提纲**

开篇点题:Giant pandas are…

正文细节描写:They live…, and they have…

结尾点题:We must try our best to…

**第三步:分层写作**

基础层:仿写句子

a symbol of ……的象征

【例句】熊猫变得如此受欢迎以至于它们现在是中国的象征。

Pandas have become so popular that they are now a symbol of China.

【仿写】大象在一些地方是好运的象征。

Elephants are a symbol of luck in some places.

try hard to 力图,全力以赴……

【例句】中国政府正全力以赴来帮助大熊猫。

The Chinese government is trying hard to help the pandas.

【仿写】一些人正全力以赴学习这些技能。

Some people are trying hard to study these skills.

提高层:扩写句子

【例句】I like giraffes.(扩写原因"因为它们是可爱的")

→I like giraffes because they are cute.

【练习】I don't like snakes.(扩写原因"因为它们太吓人")

→I don't like snakes because they are too scary.

发展层:连句成章

Giant pandas are China's national treasure. They usually live in Sichuan, Shaanxi and Gansu provinces. Giant pandas have black and white fur, and they have big eyes and round ears. Though they are fat, they move nimbly. They are really lovely animals. People love them very much. Bamboo is their favorite food. They can climb trees and swim. They usually live for 18-30 years. However, there are only a few giant pandas now. We must try hard to protect them well.

## Unit 6 I'm watching TV.

### ☞ 话题分析

本单元以“日常生活”为话题,需要学生运用现在进行时表述正在发生的动作或存在的状态。此类书面表达主要有两种题型:描写自己或自己的家庭成员在某个时候正在做的事情;根据图片描述人们正在进行的活动。

### ☞ 素材积累

【单词】

名词:newspaper 报纸 soup 汤 movie 电影 drink 饮料 tea 茶;茶水 supermarket 超市 dish 碟;盘

动词:drink 喝 shop 购物 study 学习;研究 cook 烹调;烹饪;准备(饭菜)

【短语】

read a newspaper 看报纸

make soup 煮汤

eat out 出去吃饭

drink tea 喝茶

talk on the phone 打电话

listen to a CD 听光盘

wash the dishes 洗盘子

do homework/housework 做作业/家务

【句型】

What are they doing? 他们正在做什么?

He/She is doing... 他/她正在做……

Lucy is doing... 露西正在做……

Look! They are doing... 看！他们正在做……

## ☞ 典例剖析

> 现在是晚上7点钟，格林（Green）夫人的四个孩子都在家里，她想知道他们在做什么。托尼（Tony）在客厅看电视；玛利亚（Maria）在客厅看书；西蒙（Simon）和索尼亚（Sonia）在卧室，西蒙在和狗狗玩，而索尼亚在画画。他们玩得多高兴啊！请你根据以上内容，写一篇60个词左右的短文，介绍他们正在做的事情。

**第一步：读题审题**

审
- 主题：家庭成员正在做的事
- 体裁：记叙文
- 人称：第三人称
- 时态：现在进行时

**第二步：写作提纲**

引出话题：Now it's 7 o'clock in the evening. Mrs. Green's four children...are all at home.

叙述故事：Tony's watching TV... Maria is reading a book... Simon is playing... Sonia is drawing.

总结评价：They are all happy. /What a happy family! /How happy they are!

**第三步：分层写作**

**基础层：仿写句子**

be doing sth. 正在做某事

【例句】我正在打扫我的房间。I'm cleaning my room.

【仿写】他正在打篮球。<u>He is playing basketball.</u>

提高层：扩写句子

【例句】She is exercising.（扩写时间）

→ She is exercising <u>now/on Mondays/every night/in the morning.</u>

【练习】I am reading.（扩写地点）

→ I am reading <u>at home/at school/under the tree/on the playground.</u>

发展层:连句成章

Now it's 7 o'clock in the evening. Mrs. Green's four children, Tony, Maria, Simon and Sonia are all at home. What are they doing? Well, Tony is watching TV in the living room. Maria is also in the living room. She is reading a book. Simon and Sonia are in their bedrooms. Simon is playing with his dog, while Sonia is drawing. How happy they are!

## Unit 7 It's raining!

### ☞ 话题分析

本单元谈论的话题是“天气”以及“在什么天气情况下适合做什么运动”。通过学会写电子邮件,学生需要使用“How's the weather?”“What are you doing?”“What's he/she doing?”等句式与朋友讨论彼此的假期或者活动情况。

### ☞ 素材积累

【单词】

天气:sunny 晴朗的　rainy 阴雨的;多雨的　cloudy 多云的　snowy 下雪的　windy 多风的　rainstorm 暴风雨　warm 温暖的　dry 干燥的

运动/活动:talk 说话　play 玩、弹　clean 打扫　run 跑　fish 钓鱼　read 阅读　wash 洗　take 参加(运动)　sing 唱歌　skate 滑冰　take a photo of 拍照　swim 游泳

情感:great 美妙的;好极的　good 好的;优质的　terrible 非常讨厌的;可怕的

【短语】

be happy to do sth. 很高兴做某事

have a good time doing sth. /have fun doing sth. 玩得开心

go to summer school 参加暑期学校

just right for doing sth. 正好适合干某事

be on vacation 在度假

fight with snowballs 打雪仗

**【句型】**

How's the weather in …? ……(某地)的天气怎样?

It's sunny/rainy/cold/hot. 天气晴朗/下雨/寒冷/火热。

They are having fun. 他们正玩得开心。

## ☞ 典例剖析

今天是周日,早晨阳光灿烂,在公园里有很多人,他们正在开心地玩。请你根据信息提示,写一篇60个词左右的英语短文:

1. 有一些男孩在打篮球,有些在踢足球;
2. Linda 在树下看书,Mary 在吃苹果,Frank 在与她说话;
3. Tom 和 Lucy 看着一个男孩玩耍。

**第一步:读题审题**

审
- 体裁:记叙文
- 人称:第三人称
- 时态:现在进行时
- 中心大意:关于假期

**第二步:写作提纲**

时间、地点:Sunday morning, in the park

天气状况:sunny

人物活动:some boys, play basketball, play soccer; Linda, read a book; Mary, eat apples, talk with Frank; Tom and Lucy, watch a boy playing

**第三步:分层写作**

基础层:仿写句子

just right for 正好适合

**【例句】**这儿天气凉爽又多云,正好适合散步。

The weather here is cool and cloudy, just right for walking.

**【仿写】**这种天气适合旅行。The weather is just right for travelling.

on vacation 度假

【例句】你想什么时候去度假?

When do you want to go on vacation?

【仿写】我在北京度假。I'm on vacation in Beijing.

提高层:扩写句子

【例句】There are many people.(扩写地点状语"在公园里")

→There are many people in the park.

【练习】Linda is reading a book.(扩写地点状语"在树下")

→Linda is reading a book under the tree.

I think this is a good place.(扩写不定式做定语"玩得高兴")

→I think this is a good place to have fun.

发展层:连句成章

It's sunny on Sunday morning. There are many people in the park. They spend their free time playing there happily.

Some boys are playing basketball and other boys are playing soccer ball. Linda is reading a book under the tree. Mary is eating an apple and Frank is talking to her. Tom and Lucy are watching a boy playing.

What fun they are all having!

## Unit 8 Is there a post office near here?

### ☞ 话题分析

本单元以"街区"为话题,要求学生围绕该话题谈论邻里社区的各种设施和场所位置。学生在写此类说明文时,需要灵活运用英语中"问路"和"指路"的表达方式,正确描述各种设施、建筑物的地理位置。

### ☞ 素材积累

【单词】

介词:across 过;穿过 through 穿过;贯穿 between 介于……之间 along

沿着

方位:right 向右边;右边　left 向左边;左边　east 东方;东方的　west 西方;西方的　north 北方;北方的　south 南方;南方的

建筑物:bus station 公交站　school building 教学楼　airport 机场　avenue 大街

【句型】

between...and...在……之间

go along...and turn left at the...crossing 沿着……走,在……十字路口左转

There is... 有一个……

The...is across from... ……在……对面

## ☞ 典例剖析

假如你是李明,你收到了美国朋友 Robin 的来信,他将于 12 月 15 日和他妹妹一起到北京来看望你。但碰巧你那时在珠海有个会议,无法接他们。为此,你回信向 Robin 表示歉意,并告诉他从机场如何到你家。首先,出机场坐 359 路公交车到东直门。然后,步行经过东直门立交桥(flyover),往西边走,在右边有个书店,然后左转再直行。最后,在右边可以看到一个公园和一家银行,左边是一家电影院,你家紧挨着电影院。找到 403 室,你母亲那时会在家中迎接他们。在信的末尾你告诉他们,你将于 12 月 17 日回北京。

要求:

1. 短文必须包括文字说明的所有要点。

2. 短文必须按文中所给的交通路线和交通方式做出说明。

**第一步:读题审题**

审
- 体裁:说明文
- 人称:第一人称;第二人称
- 时态:一般现在时
- 句型:there be 句型

**第二步:写作提纲**

开头句(引入话题):I'm writing to tell you the way to...

正文(重点介绍方位):You can walk from…then go along… go straight and soon…

结尾(简洁祝愿):I hope you have a…

**第三步:分层写作**

基础层:仿写句子

go along 沿着

**【例句】**沿着中央大街走,你就会找到它。

Go along Center Street and you'll find it.

**【仿写】**为了早点到那,我顺着长街走并在街口左转。

To get there earlier, I walk along the Long Street and turn left at the corner.

on the right 在右边

**【例句】**车站在右边。The station is on the right.

**【仿写】**我家在右边,图书馆隔壁。

My home is on the right, next to the library.

提高层:扩写句子

**【例句】**Your sister is coming to Beijing.(扩写时间状语"在 12 月 15 日")

→Your sister is coming to Beijing on December 15th.

**【练习】**I'm sorry that I can't meet you.(扩写原因"因为我在珠海有个会议")

→I'm sorry that I can't meet you because I have a meeting in Zhuhai.

发展层:连句成章

Dear Robin,

I'm very glad that you and your sister are coming to Beijing and visit me on December 15th. But I'm sorry that I can't meet you that day because I have a meeting in Zhuhai. Now let me tell you how to get to my home.

When you get out of the airport, you can take Bus 359 to Dongzhimen. Walk across the Dongzhimen Flyover and go to the west. You can see a book shop on your right. Turn left and go straight. You can see a park and a bank on your right, and then a cinema on your left. My home is next to the cinema. Find Room 403 and my mother will meet you at home.

I will be back on December 17th.

Yours,

Li Ming

## Unit 9 What does he look like?

### ☞ 话题分析

本单元以"描述人的外貌"为话题,需要学生通过使用外貌相关的词汇和句型,对一个人的外貌、特征、体型等方面进行描述。体裁以说明文为主,时态多涉及一般现在时,人称常使用第三人称单数,写作模式多为三段式。

### ☞ 素材积累

【单词】

身高:height 身高;高度　tall 高的

体型:thin 瘦的;苗条的　heavy 重的;胖的

头发:long 长的　short 短的　curly 卷曲的　straight 直的　blonde 金黄色的

其他特征相关:glasses 眼镜　jeans 牛仔裤　sports shoes 运动鞋

【短语】

look like 看起来像

of medium height/build 中等身高/身材

wear glasses 戴眼镜

be good at 擅长于

like to do 喜欢做某事

first of all 首先

【句型】

my best friend is... 我最好的朋友是……

Let me tell you what he/she looks like. 让我来告诉你他/她长什么样。

he/she usually wears... 他/她通常穿……

I like him/her because… 我喜欢他/她因为……

he/she is good at… 他/她擅长于……

## ☞ 典例剖析

请你写一篇60个词左右的短文,描述一下你的好友 Lanlan,以“My Best Friend”为题,内容要点包括:

1. 兰州人,年龄13岁;
2. 体型:瘦高、圆脸,喜欢穿牛仔裤、戴帽子;
3. 喜欢唱歌;
4. 身材中等;
5. 因为她很善良,所以我喜欢她。

注意:1. 文中须包含所给内容要点,条理清晰、行文连贯,可适当发挥;

2. 文中不能出现真实的人名和校名等信息。

**第一步:读题审题**

审:
- 体裁:说明文
- 人称:第三人称
- 时态:一般现在时
- 段落:三段式(总—分—总)

**第二步:写作提纲**

第一段:点明要介绍的人物。My friend… is a beautiful girl/is a handsome boy.

第二段:描述外貌和服饰。She/He is thin/of medium height… She/he has short straight hair/has big eyes … She/he never wears… She/he likes wearing jeans…

第三段:总述。I like her/him because…

**第三步:分层写作**

基础层:仿写句子

what sb. look(s) like 某人长相……

【例句】让我说说他的长相。Let me tell what he looks like.

【仿写】你爸长什么样？What does your father look like?

wear jeans 穿牛仔裤

【例句】Lisa 从来不穿牛仔裤。

Lisa never wears jeans.

【仿写】我们的英语老师总是穿牛仔裤。

Our English teacher always wears jeans.

提高层：扩写句子

【例句】Let me tell...（扩写告诉的内容“他长什么样子”）

→Let me tell what he looks like.

【练习】I like him.（扩写原因“因为他酷且有趣”）

→I like him because he is cool and fun.

发展层：连句成章

My Best Friend

My best friend is Lanlan. Now let me tell what she looks like. Lanlan is a 13-year-old girl. She is from Lanzhou. She is thin and tall. She has a round face, two big eyes and looks very cute. She likes singing songs. She is of medium build. She likes to wear jeans and a cap. I like her because she is kind.

## Unit 10 I'd like some noodles.

### ☞ 话题分析

本单元以“订餐与就餐”为话题，需要学生学会表达自己的就餐意向。学生的学习目标有两点：①能够掌握“订餐与就餐”的方式、方法；②能够自如地将所学句型运用到实际交流中。作文中的人称应该为第一人称，时态为一般现在时。学生在写了自己喜欢的食物后，要说明这些食物对自己的身体有没有好处，以及应该怎样合理饮食。

## ☞ 素材积累

【单词】

肉类:beef 牛肉　chicken 鸡肉　mutton 羊肉　meat(可食用的)肉

菜类:carrot 胡萝卜　tomato 西红柿　cabbage 卷心菜　potato 土豆;马铃薯

水果类:orange 橙子;柑橘　strawberry 草莓　apple 苹果　pear 梨

banana 香蕉

饮料:green tea 绿茶　orange juice 橙汁　water 水　milk 牛奶

其他:pancake 烙饼;薄饼　dumpling 饺子　porridge 粥　hamburger 汉堡包

【短语】

would like 想要

one large bowl of 一大碗

be/get popular 受欢迎

【句型】

What kind of…? 哪种……?

Would you like…? 你想要……?

What size…? 多大……?

You can try our… 你可以尝尝我们的……

It is very good/delicious. 它很好/美味。

## ☞ 典例剖析

> 请根据下面的汉语提示,为店主写一则小广告,词数不少于 60 个。
>
> 科学院小学门口右边开了一家饺子馆(dumpling house),现新上四种很好吃的特色饺子:①牛肉芹菜(celery)馅饺子;②羊肉胡萝卜馅饺子;③蔬菜馅饺子;④鸡蛋豆腐馅饺子。有大碗、中碗、小碗三种。店内还有果汁、可乐和绿茶。

**第一步:读题审题**

审{
- 体裁:应用文
- 人称:第一人称
- 时态:一般现在时

**第二步:写作提纲**

第一段:欢迎到饺子馆进餐。Welcome to…! What kind of dumplings would you like? We have great new special dumplings…

第二段:给出具体信息。①介绍四种特色饺子。beef and celery dumplings, mutton and carrot dumplings, vegetable dumplings, eggs and toufu dumplings ②介绍大中小碗类别以及其他特色食品。We have large, medium and small bowls of dumplings; we also have juice, coke and green tea.

第三段:号召大家亲自来看看。Come and see for yourself at our dumpling house.

**第三步:分层写作**

*基础层:仿写句子*

Would you like…? 你要来些……?

【例句】你要来些饺子吗? Would you like some dumplings?

【仿写】你要喝点橙子汁吗? Would you like some orange juice?

have…for… 为……准备好……

【例句】我们为你准备好了各种食品。

We have kinds of food for you.

【仿写】我们也为你准备好了绿茶。We also have green tea for you.

*提高层:扩写句子*

【例句】Welcome to… (扩写地点"我们的饺子馆")

→Welcome to our dumpling house.

【练习】Come and see. (扩写状语"亲自")

→Come and see for yourself.

*发展层:连句成章*

Welcome to our dumpling house! What kind of dumplings would you like? We have four great new special dumplings:

①beef and celery dumplings;

②mutton and carrot dumplings;

③vegetable dumplings;

④eggs and toufu dumplings.

We have large, medium and small bowls of dumplings. We also have juice, coke and green tea.

Come and see for yourself at our dumpling house!

## Unit 11 How was your school trip?

### ☞ 话题分析

本单元以“日记”为话题,要求学生学会写英文日记,在日记中叙述过去发生的事情。人称一般用第一人称;时态通常用一般过去时。写作时要注意日记格式,写清楚时间、天气状况以及自己的感受。具体来说,日记中应包含:

①What was the date?

②Where did you go?

③How was the trip?

④How did you go there?

⑤What did you see? /What did you do?

⑥Did you like it?

### ☞ 素材积累

**【单词】**

天气:rainy 多雨的;阴雨连绵的 cloudy 多云的 sunny 晴朗的 snowy 下雪的

星期:Monday 星期一 Tuesday 星期二 Wednesday 星期三 Thursday 星期四 Friday 星期五 Saturday 星期六 Sunday 星期天

**【短语】**

go on a school trip 参加一次学校(组织的)短途旅行

by train 坐火车

learn about 了解

make a model robot 制作一个模型机器人

take photos of … 为……拍照

buy…for… 给……买……

take a train 乘火车

be interested in…对……感兴趣

【句型】

It was an exciting day. 那是令人激动的一天。

I'm not interested in that. 我对那个不感兴趣。

It was difficult to take photos. 拍照很难。

We had a great time yesterday. 昨天我们玩得很开心。

## ☞ 典例剖析

请根据下面的内容提示写一篇英语日记,描述你们去农场郊游的经历。

内容提示:

1. 上周六,你们骑自行车去阳光农场(Sunshine Farm)郊游。
2. 上午你们给奶牛挤奶、喂鸡,还摘了新鲜的(fresh)蔬菜。
3. 下午你们在农场散步,和农场的农民聊天。
4. 你们玩得很开心。

注意:词数不少于60个。符合日记格式。

**第一步:读题审题**

审
- 体裁:记叙文(日记)
- 时态:一般过去时
- 人称:第一人称

**第二步:思维导图**

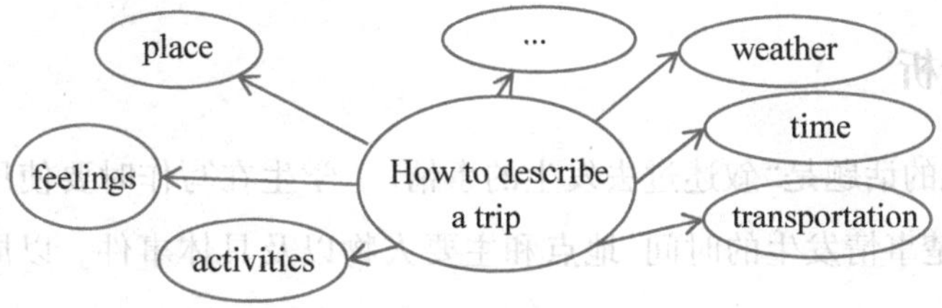

**第三步:分层写作**

基础层:仿写句子

milk a cow/cows 挤牛奶

**【例句】**她刚刚挤牛奶了。She milked a cow just now.

**【仿写】**我们一起去农场挤牛奶了。

We went to a farm to milk cows together.

feed chickens 喂鸡

**【例句】**妈妈每天喂鸡。Mom feeds chickens every day.

**【仿写】**我们在农场里喂鸡。We feed chickens in the farm.

提高层:扩写句子

**【例句】**We went to the Sunshine Farm.(扩写出行方式"乘火车")

→We went to the Sunshine Farm by train.

**【练习】**We also went to the field.(扩写目的状语"摘些新鲜蔬菜")

→We also went to the field to pick some fresh vegetables.

发展层:连句成章

Last Saturday we had a great school trip. We went to the Sunshine Farm by bike. In the morning, we milked cows and fed chickens. We also went to the field to pick some fresh vegetables. It was interesting. In the afternoon, we went for a walk on the farm. We talked with the farmer and he told us something about the farm. We learned a lot and we had a good time on the farm. We were tired but happy.

## Unit 12 What did you do last weekend?

### ☞ 话题分析

本单元的话题是"叙述过去发生的事情"。学生在写作时要使用一般过去时,交代清楚事情发生的时间、地点和主要人物以及具体事件。以周末活动为例,可采用"总—分—总"写法。

## ☞ 素材积累

【单词】

活动相关词汇:busy 忙碌的  terrible 可怕的  relaxing 令人放松的  exciting 使人兴奋的;令人激动的  weekend 周末  visit 参观;拜访  tired 疲劳的

【短语】

时间相关短语:

on Saturday morning 在周六上午

on Saturday afternoon 在周六下午

on Saturday night 在周六晚上

on Sunday morning 在周日上午

on Sunday afternoon 在周日下午

on Sunday night 在周日晚上

其他短语:

go boating 去划船

go to the beach 去海滩

visit grandparents 看望爷爷奶奶/姥姥姥爷

fly a kite 放风筝

study for a test 备考;为考试学习

visit a museum 参观一家博物馆

【句型】

I had a…weekend and I did many things. 我度过了一个……周末,做了许多事。

That's why…but… 那就是……的原因,但是……

How interesting it is! 多么有趣的一天啊!

## ☞ 典例剖析

请你根据下面的提示写一篇文章,描述上周日发生的一件事情:

①你下午去看电影;

②你遇到了一个正在角落里哭泣的小女孩;

③你想帮助她,于是把她带到了派出所(police station);

④在派出所正好遇到了小女孩的妈妈。

要求:1. 60 个词左右;

2. 条理清晰,层次分明。

**第一步:读题审题**

审
- 体裁:记叙文
- 主题:过去发生的事
- 人称:第一人称
- 时态:一般过去时

**第二步:写作提纲**

第一段:交代时间、地点。It was sunny last Sunday… I went to the movies…

第二段:描述具体经过。I found a little girl crying at the corner. …went up to her and asked her… I decided to send her to the police station.

第三段:…I was very happy/delighted/excited…

**第三步:分层写作**

基础层:仿写句子

do one's homework 做作业

**【例句】**上周末我在家做作业。I did my homework at home last weekend.

**【仿写】**约翰即使在周末也做作业。

John did his homework even on the weekend.

feel / find / see / hear sb. / sth. doing sth. 感觉到 / 发现 / 看到 / 听到某人 / 某物在做某事

**【例句】**我能感觉到有东西在我背上动。

I can feel things moving on my back.

【仿写】我发现一个小女孩在哭。I found a girl crying.

提高层:扩写句子

【例句】Her mother left.(扩写时间状语"当我们到达那儿")

→Her mother left when we got there.

【练习】I found a little girl crying.(扩写状语"在拐角处")

→I found a little girl crying at the corner.

发展层:连句成章

It was sunny last Sunday. I went to the movies in the afternoon.

Near the cinema, I found a little girl crying at the corner. I went up to her and asked her what was wrong. She didn't know her home address, so I sent her to the police station. When we got there, her mother was already there. How happy they were!

I missed the movie, but I was very happy.

## 第三节 八年级上册

经过七年级的学习,学生的写作素养会有很大提高,所以八年级上学期,教师对学生的写作要求也随之提高。基础层的主要任务是选词填空(根据语境,用所给词或短语的正确形式填空,使句意通顺。),选词的难度并不大;提高层的主要任务是根据括号内所给信息填空;发展层的主要任务是根据指令完成任务。

### Unit 1 Where did you go on vacation?

#### ☞ 话题分析

本单元的写作体裁为日记。日记是具有记叙文性质的应用文,需要学生将一天中所经历的主要事情和对应的感受依次简要地记下来。

**基本框架:**

第一段:开头段,交代时间(time)、地点(place)、人物(character)、事件

(business)和天气(weather)。

第二段:正文,介绍活动和感受。We did/heard/ate/enjoyed/thought…

第三段:一天结束后的感受。I feel/felt…

**写作范例**

Wednesday, August 20th

**Beginning**: Today's weather was hot and sunny. I went to a Beijing Hutong. It was beautiful.

**Main body**: I took some photos. I liked this place because I learned something important. For dinner I had Beijing roast duck. It was delicious.

**Ending**: In the evening, I felt really tired.

## ☞ 典例剖析

假如你是李华,这个暑假你和你父母一起去了北京,你们在北京游览了很多地方。请你以"My Trip to Beijing"为题,写一篇短文,记述你的这次旅行。

参考词汇:the flag-raising ceremony 升旗仪式; the Palace Museum 故宫博物院; the Summer Palace 颐和园; the Temple of Heaven 天坛

要求:1. 文中不得出现任何真实的人名、校名及其他相关信息;

2. 不少于70个词。

**写作点拨:**

话题:旅游

时态:一般过去时

人称:第一人称

体裁:记叙文

**句型荟萃:**

Read ten thousand books and travel ten thousand miles. 读万卷书,行万里路。

He who travels far knows much. 见多识广。

分层写作:

基础层:根据语境,用所给词或短语的正确形式填空,使句意通顺。

| photo | play | something | make | visit |
|---|---|---|---|---|

My Trip to Beijing

Wednesday, August 1st

This summer vacation, I went to Beijing with my parents. We had a good time there.

We visited many places of interest, such as the Palace Museum, the Summer Palace, the Temple of Heaven and so on. On Tian'anmen Square, we watched the flag-raising ceremony, which made us excited. Besides, today is the China's Army Day. So there were many people and the Square was very crowded. We had great fun playing there! Then we went to visit the Great Wall. How great it is! I took many photos there. At last, we traveled around Beijing Hutong on three-wheels; it was very interesting. There is no doubt that we had Beijing roast duck for dinner. Everything was excellent there.

Tired as we were, we were so delighted that we felt like visiting Beijing again.

提高层:根据括号内所给信息填空。

My Trip to Beijing

Wednesday, August 1st

This summer vacation, I went to Beijing with my parents. We had a good time (我们玩得高兴) there.

We visited many places of interest(名胜), such as the Palace Museum, the Summer Palace, the Temple of Heaven and so on. On Tian'anmen Square, we watched the flag-raising ceremony, which made us excited(使我们非常激动). Besides, today is the China's Army Day. So there were many people and the square was very crowded. We had great fun playing(玩得非常快乐) there! Then we went to visit the Great Wall. How great it is! I took many photos(拍了许多照片) there.

At last, we traveled around Beijing Hutong on three-wheels; it was very interesting. There is no doubt that we had Beijing roast duck for dinner. Everything was excellent (一切都是那么美好) there.

Tired as we were, we were so delighted that we felt like visiting Beijing again.

发展层:根据指令完成任务。

My Trip to Beijing

Wednesday, August 1st

This summer vacation, I went to Beijing with my parents. We had a good time there.

We visited many places of interest, such as the Palace Museum, the Summer Palace, the Temple of Heaven and so on. On Tian'anmen Square, ①we watched the flag-raising ceremony, and it made us excited. Besides, today is the China's Army Day. So there were many people and the squere was very crowded. We had great fun playing there! Then we went to visit the Great Wall. How great it is! I took many photos there. At last, we traveled around Beijing Hutong on three-wheels; it was very interesting. ②There is no doubt that we had Beijing roast duck for dinner. Everything was excellent there.

Tired as we were, we were so delighted that we felt like visiting Beijing again.

1. 将①处画线句子用 which 合并为非限制性定语从句。

we watched the flag-raising ceremony, which made us excited

2. 将②处画线句子改为其同义句。

We had Beijing roast duck for dinner without doubt

## Unit 2 How often do you exercise?

### ☞ 话题分析

本单元的话题是"介绍自己的健康生活方式"。学生可以从锻炼、饮食以及空闲时间的活动这三方面来介绍自己的好习惯。写作时要注意频率副词的使用，开头和结尾要点题，强调健康生活方式的重要性。

**基本框架：**

第一段：引出话题。Everyone has his own habits. Here are my good and bad habits.

第二段：介绍习惯。（好习惯）I have a lot of good habits. I drink milk every day and I usually…；I like…I go to…Also, I never…/I hardly ever…/I often…（坏习惯）However, I have some bad habits, too. I never…/I hardly ever…and I always…

第三段：表明决心。Old habits die hard. So I will start changing before it's too late.

## ☞ 典例剖析

> 假如你是八年六班的李华，你校校报拟举办主题为“健康生活方式”的征文活动，以此来宣传健康生活的知识，倡导健康的生活方式，引导学生养成健康的生活习惯。请你写一篇不少于70个词的英语短文进行投稿，介绍你自己的健康生活方式。
>
> 要点提示：
>
> 1. 锻炼：每天早晨跑步，每周和朋友踢足球两次；
> 2. 饮食：每天早晨喝牛奶，多吃蔬菜和水果，从不吃垃圾食品；
> 3. 空闲时间：读书和杂志，很少玩电脑游戏。

**写作点拨：**

话题：日常活动

时态：一般现在时

人称：第一人称

**句型荟萃：**

It's bad for health. 这对健康不利。

I love reading books and magazines. 我喜欢读书和杂志。

I sleep for at least eight hours every day. 我每天至少睡八个小时。

Healthy lifestyle is good for my mind and body. 健康的生活方式对我的身心

有益。

**分层写作：**

基础层：根据语境，用所给词或短语的正确形式填空，使句意通顺。

| | | | | | | | | | |
|---|---|---|---|---|---|---|---|---|---|
| vegetable | exercise | for | hour | little | two | magazine | eat | hard | healthy |

Hello, everyone! I'm Li Hua from Class 6, Grade 8. I have a healthy lifestyle. I often exercise. Every morning, I run for half an hour, and I play soccer with my friends twice a week. I also have good eating habits. I drink some milk every morning, and I eat a lot of fruit and vegetables. But I never have junk food because it's bad for health. In my free time, I hardly ever play computer games. I love reading books and magazines. I sleep for at least eight hours every night. Healthy lifestyle is good for both my mind and my body.

提高层：根据括号内所给信息填空。

Hello, everyone! I'm Li Hua from Class 6, Grade 8. I have a healthy lifestyle. I often exercise(我经常锻炼). Every morning, I run for half an hour, and I play soccer with my friends twice a week(我和我朋友一周踢两次足球). I also have good eating habits. I drink some milk every morning, and I eat a lot of fruit and vegetables. But I never have junk food because it's bad for health (因为对健康有害). In my free time, I hardly ever play computer games(几乎不玩电脑游戏). I love reading books and magazines. I sheep for at least eight hours (至少睡八小时) every night. Healthy lifestyle is good for both my mind and my body.

发展层：根据指令完成任务。

Hello, everyone! I'm Li Hua from Class 6, Grade 8. I have a healthy lifestyle. I often exercise. Every morning, I run for half an hour, and I play soccer with my friends twice a week. ① I also have good eating habits. I drink some milk every morning, and I eat a lot of fruit and vegetables. But I never have junk food because it's bad for health. ② In my free time, I hardly ever play computer games. I love reading books and magazines. I sleep for at least eight hours every night. Healthy lifestyle is good for both my mind and my body.

1. 将①处句子改为其同义句：

I have good eating habits, too. /I have good eating habits as well.

2. 将②处句子用“It is…that…”句式改写。

It is in my free time that I hardly ever play computer games.

## Unit 3 I'm more outgoing than my sister.

### ☞ 话题分析

本单元的话题是比较自己与朋友。学生需要从性格、外貌、爱好和品质等方面介绍自己的好朋友。介绍发型时，可用“He/She has… hair”；介绍爱好时，可用“He/She likes…”；其他可用“be+形容词”，适当运用 and 及 but 增加内容的连贯性。作文多采用“三段式”：第一段简单介绍朋友；第二段介绍自己与朋友的异同；第三段介绍自己对朋友的看法。

**基本框架**：

第一段：引出人物。…is my good/best friend.

第二段：自己与朋友的异同。可从外貌、爱好、个性等方面介绍。We are both… I'm (not) as…as… I'm…than…/be better at…；… is different from me in…

第三段：对朋友的看法。… like him/her … because I am lucky to have a friend…；…always bring out the best in me/always there to care about me.

### ☞ 典例剖析

在你的初中生活中，你总会与一些人成为朋友。请你以“My Best Friend and I”为题，根据以下提示，写一篇不少于 70 个词的短文。

提示：

1. Who is your best friend?

2. How are you the same as and different from your best friend?

3. What do you like about him/her?

**写作点拨:**

时态:一般现在时

人称:第一人称;第三人称

体裁:记叙文

**句型荟萃:**

A good friend is like a mirror. 好朋友就像一面镜子。

Friends are like books — you don't need a lot of them as long as they're good. 朋友就像书——你不需要很多,只要他们是好的。

My best friend helps to bring out the best in me. 我最好的朋友帮助我展露出我最好的一面。

A true friend reaches for your hand and touches your heart. 一个真正的朋友(在你需要时)向你伸出援手,使你感动。

**分层写作:**

基础层:根据语境,用所给词或短语的正确形式填空,使句意通顺。

| | | | | |
|---|---|---|---|---|
| smart | play | look like | grade | bring out |

### My Best Friend and I

Mary is my best friend. Some people think we are sisters because she looks like me. We both have long curly hair and big eyes. We are both outgoing and hard-working, but I think she is smarter than me because she always gets better grades than I do. We both like ping-pong. Mary is really good at playing ping-pong, so she always wins.

However, she often helps to bring out the best in me. Now I am getting better at ping-pong.

Mary is smart and kind. I am so lucky to have a friend like her.

提高层:根据括号内所给信息填空。

### My Best Friend and I

Mary is my best friend. Some people think we are sisters because she looks like me（因为她看起来像我）. We both have long curly hair and big eyes. We are both outgoing and hard-working, but I think she is smarter than me（她比我聪明）because she always gets better grades than I do. We both like ping-pong. Mary is really good at playing（真的擅长打）ping-pong, so she always wins.

However, she often helps to bring out the best in me（展露出我最好的一面）. Now I am getting better at ping-pong.

Mary is smart and kind. I am so lucky to have a friend like her.

发展层：根据指令完成任务。

## My Best Friend and I

Mary is my best friend. ①Some people think we are sisters because she looks like me. We both have long curly hair and big eyes. We are both outgoing and hard-working, but I think she is smarter than me because she always gets better grades than I do. ②We both like ping-pong. Mary is really good at playing ping-pong, so she always wins.

However, ③she often helps to bring out the best in me. Now I am getting better at ping-pong.

④Mary is smart and kind. I am so lucky to have a friend like her.

1. 将①处句子改为"it is+原因状语+that..."。

It is because she looks like me that some people think we are sisters.

2. 将②处句子用"not only...but also..."改写。

Not only she but also I like ping-pong.

3. 将③处句子用 do anything that sb. can to do 句型改写。

she often does anything that she can to help to bring out the best in me.

4. 将④处句子用"so...that..."结构改写。

I am so lucky that I have a friend like Mary, who is smart and kind.

## Unit 4 What's the best movie theater?

### ☞ 话题分析

本单元的写作话题为“介绍自己居住地的最好的地方或事物,并说明原因”。学生可以先描述最好/喜欢的某个地方,然后说明原因,注意要用形容词或副词的最高级形式来描述。

**基本框架:**

1. 先介绍自己喜欢的地方或者事物。

The best places/things in my town… the best school/park/restaurant/library/supermarket/shopping mall/movie theater/clothes store…

2. 再阐述自己喜欢某地或某事物的原因。

Reason: distance(far/close), area(big/large/small), service(good/friendly), quality(good), price(low/high), products(delicious/fresh), popularity(popular/famous), convenience(convenient/quick), environment(clean/quiet/beautiful), location(on…street)…

### ☞ 典例剖析

假如你是李华,你校校报拟举办主题为“我爱我的家乡”的征文活动,以此来为家乡做宣传。请你写一篇 80 个词左右的英语短文进行投稿,介绍你自己喜欢的学校、餐馆、饮食、购物中心等并说明原因。

要求:书写规范,要点齐全。

**写作点拨:**

时态:一般现在时

人称:第一人称;第三人称

体裁:说明文

**句型荟萃:**

I live in a beautiful city. 我住在一个美丽的城市。

My city has the…, the best…is…because… 我的城市有……,最好的……

是……因为……

**分层写作：**

基础层：根据语境，用所给词或短语的正确形式填空，使句意通顺。

| clothes | beautiful | shop | quality | find | food | good |
|---|---|---|---|---|---|---|

My name is Li Hua. Now I live in a beautiful city near the Yellow River. The best and the most beautiful high school here is the one attached to Northwest Normal University. The best supermarket is WP because it has the best quality things and the best service. The best restaurant is K because it has the most delicious food and it is the cleanest restaurant. The best clothes store is BA because it has the best quality clothes and it has the most beautiful shopping environment. The most famous food is beef noodles in my city because it has a unique taste and there is nowhere to find this special flavor.

Such is my city. Welcome here!

提高层：根据括号内所给信息填空。

My name is Li Hua. Now I live in a beautiful city near the Yellow River. The best and the most beautiful high school here（这里最好、最美丽的高中）is the one attached to Northwest Normal University. The best supermarket is WP because it has the best quality things and the best service（最好的服务）. The best restaurant is K because it has the most delicious food and it is the cleanest restaurant. The best clothes store is BA because it has the best quality clothes and it has the most beautiful shopping environment（有最优美的购物环境）. The most famous food is beef noodles in my city because it has a unique taste and there is nowhere to find（任何地方找不到）this special flavor.

Such is my city. Welcome here!

发展层：根据指令完成任务。

My name is Li Hua. Now I live in a beautiful city ①near the Yellow River. The best and the most beautiful high school here is the one attached to Northwest Normal University. The best supermarket is WP because it has the best quality things and the best service. The best restaurant is K because it has the most delicious food and it is the cleanest restaurant. The best clothes store is BA because ②it has the best quality clothes and it has the most beautiful shopping environment. The most famous food is beef noodles in my city because it has a unique taste and there is nowhere to find this special flavor.

Such is my city. Welcome here!

1. 将①处句子改为“黄河穿城而过”(用定语从句)。

...which the Yellow River runs through

2. 将②处句子用“not only...but also...”合并为一句。

...it has not only the best quality clothes but also the most beautiful shopping environment.

## Unit 5 Do you want to watch a game show?

### ☞ 话题分析

本单元的写作主题是“写影评”。影评,即电影评论,属于夹叙夹议的议论文,是对一部电影的导演、演员、摄影、剧情、环境等进行的分析和评论。影评的写作主要涉及以下几个方面:影片的名称、类型,故事发生的背景,故事的情节、社会影响力,以及自己对这部影片的评价。学生在写此类文章时,时态应用一般现在时与一般过去时。在内容的安排上,首先,可介绍影片的类型及主角等;然后,介绍故事的梗概;最后,表达自己对该影片的看法。

基本框架:

第一段:引出话题。

Many people like to..., they think it's... However, different people like...; Do you like...? /There are more and more... recently, such as...; different people have different preferences on movies.

第二段:主体内容。

1. 表示喜欢。like/love doing sth. /to do sth. ; enjoy sth. /doing sth. ; be fond of sth. /doing sth. ; be interested in sth.

2. 表示不喜欢。Don't like/dislike sth. /doing sth. ; hate sth. /to do sth. ; can't

stand sth.

3. 表示观点。…like(s)…best because he/she thinks/believes…; as for…, he/she…because…; in…'s eyes,… is the best movie because…

第三段:总结观点,发出号召。

## ☞ 典例剖析

> 假如你是李明。你的英语老师要求你明天在英语课上讲述你对电影《哪吒之魔童降世》的感受。请你今晚观看《哪吒之魔童降世》,为明天英语课上的精彩发言做好准备。
>
> 要求:1. 80个词左右;2. 观点合理、逻辑严谨、语句通顺。

**写作点拨:**

时态:一般现在时

人称:第一人称

体裁:议论文

**分层写作:**

基础层:根据语境,用所给词或短语的正确形式填空,使句意通顺。

| | | | | | | | | | |
|---|---|---|---|---|---|---|---|---|---|
| be | figure | movie | believe | fantastic | cartoon | save | become | excite | act |

*Ne Zha: Birth of the Demon Child* is an exciting cartoon movie.

The movie is about a famous figure named Ne Zha in Chinese ancient mythology. In the movie, Ne Zha was born to be magic. But he didn't accept his fate. He believed he was the master of his own fate. With the help of his master and parents, he tried his best to save people in danger. At last, he became a great hero.

I enjoy the movie very much. I think it is a fantastic movie with a lot of good action scenes. If you like Chinese ancient mythology and cartoons, you should watch this movie.

提高层:根据括号内所给信息填空。

*Ne Zha: Birth of the Demon Child* is an exciting cartoon movie.

The movie is about a famous figure named (取名) Ne Zha in Chinese ancient mythology. In the movie, Ne Zha was born to be magic. But he didn't accept his fate (接受他的命运). He believed he was the master of his own fate. With the help of (在……的帮助下) his master and parents, he tried his best to save people in danger (处于危险之中). At last, he became a great hero.

I enjoy the movie very much. I think it is a fantastic movie with a lot of good action scenes (有许多不错的武打场景). If you like Chinese ancient mythology and cartoons, you should watch this movie.

发展层:根据指令完成任务。

*Ne Zha: Birth of the Demon Child* is an exciting cartoon movie.

The movie is about a famous figure ①named Ne Zha in Chinese ancient mythology. In the movie, Ne Zha was born to be magic. But he didn't accept his fate. He believed he was the master of his own fate. With the help of his master and parents, ② he tried his best to save people in danger. At last, he became a great hero.

I enjoy the movie very much. I think it is a fantastic movie with a lot of good action scenes. If you like Chinese ancient mythology and cartoons, you should watch this movie.

1. 将①处改为定语从句:

"...who/that was named Ne Zha"或"whose name was Ne Zha"

2. 将②处改为其同义句。

"he did his best to save people in danger"或"he went all out of the way to save people in danger"或"he spared no effort to save people in danger"或"he did all he could to save people in danger"

## Unit 6 I'm going to study computer science.

### ☞ 话题分析

本单元的写作主题是"新年计划"。学生写作时可采用三段式:第一段引出话题,表述自己的计划;第二段针对不同的计划写出不同的实现方式;第三段谈谈自己对自己的期望。

**基本框架：**

第一段：引出话题。

Resolutions can make you a better person and make your life easier. I'm going to make…resolutions.

第二段：实现方式。

1. 分层描述自己的几种决心，写出"是什么，怎么做，为什么"。

The first resolution is about sth./doing sth./how to do sth.

I'm going to…I want/plan/hope/expect to…

(because)…be good for/help…

2. 分层有序，衔接自然。

使用 and、also、too、first、second、then、after that 等起到一定连接作用的词或短语；使用"As for my parents/my friends…"等能够引起下文的表述。

第三段：表达期望，总结点题。

I think if/as long as I try my best to make the resolutions come true, my life will be more wonderful and meaningful.

## ☞ 典例剖析

2025 年离我们越来越近，你对 2024 年有什么感受？你做好了迎接 2025 年来临的准备了吗？请你以"My New Year's Resolutions"为题写一篇文章，向校报投稿。内容包括新年计划、实现新年计划的方式，以及对 2025 年的期待。

写作要求：

1. 不能照抄课本原文；不得在作文中出现真实姓名、校名等；

2. 语句连贯，注意分段，80 个词左右。

**写作点拨：**

时态：一般将来时

人称：第一人称

体裁：说明文

**短语储备：**

improve our lives 改善我们的生活

start an exercise program 启动一个锻炼计划

take up a hobby 培养一项爱好

keep resolutions 坚持计划

**分层写作：**

基础层：根据语境，用所给词或短语的正确形式填空，使句意通顺。

| | | | | | | | | | |
|---|---|---|---|---|---|---|---|---|---|
| true | improve | much | hard | relationship | take | grade | practice | health | swim |

### My New Year's Resolutions

New Year is coming. I'm going to do a lot of things next year.

First, I want to improve my English, so I'm going to practice it very hard and have many conversations with my English friends. Then, I want to take part in the sports meeting and get good grades, so I'm going to do sports every day, such as swimming and running. At the same time, I'm going to eat healthy food instead of junk food. Next, I want to join the dancing club, so I'm going to practice dancing twice a week. Finally, I want to improve my relationships with my family. I'm going to spend more time with them on weekends and talk with them more often.

I hope my resolutions can come true in 2025.

提高层：根据括号内所给信息填空。

### My New Year's Resolutions

New Year is coming. I'm going to do a lot of things next year.

First, I want to improve my English, so I'm going to practice it（我打算练习它）very hard and have many conversations with my English friends. Then, I want to take part in the sports meeting and get good grades（取得好成绩）, so I'm going to do sports every day（每天体育锻炼）, such as swimming and running. At the same time, I'm going to eat healthier food instead of junk food. Next, I want to join the dancing club, so I'm going to practice dancing twice a week（一周练两次跳舞）.

Finally, I want to improve my relationships with my family. I'm going to spend more time with them on weekends and talk with them more often.

I hope my resolutions can come true(我的计划能够实现) in 2025.

发展层:根据指令完成任务。

### My New Year's Resolutions

New Year is coming. I'm going to do a lot of things next year.

First, I want to improve my English, so I'm going to practice it very hard and have many conversations with my English friends. Then, I want to take part in the sports meeting and get good grades, so I'm going to do sports every day, ①such as swimming and running. At the same time, I'm going to eat healthier food instead of junk food. Next, I want to join the dancing club, so I'm going to practice dancing twice a week. Finally, ②I want to improve my relationships with my family. I'm going to spend more time with them on weekends and talk with them more often.

I hope ③my resolutions can come true in 2025.

1. 根据上下文将①处内容用 for example 改换为句子。

...for example, I'm going to swim and run.

2. 将②处句子用"it is+介词短语+that..."结构改写为强调句。

...it is with my family that I want to improve my relationships.

3. 将③处画线部分改为其同义句。

...I can realize my resolutions in 2025.

## Unit 7 Will people have robots?

### ☞ 话题分析

本单元的写作主题是"根据自己的想象描述未来的事物"。这类文章的要求往往很明确,给出的提示也很具体。介绍未来的事物时,多用一般将来时进行描述,且多用表示将来时的时间状语。

**基本框架：**

第一段：引出话题。In 10/20/30 ... years，I will ...；my school/life/family will...

第二段：具体描述。I will work/travel/live...

第三段：提出期望。I'm sure I will have a/an...life.

## ☞ 典例剖析

> 校团委正在举行“畅想未来”的征文活动，请根据提示，以“My Ideal School Life”为题，写一篇短文。
>
> 内容包括：1. 简要描述现在的校园生活；2. 理想的校园生活包括理想的课后活动、学习方式、人际关系、校外生活等。
>
> 要求：1. 不得出现真实的人名、校名、地名等相关信息；
>
> 2. 80 个词左右。

**写作点拨：**

时态：一般将来时

人称：第一人称

体裁：记叙文

**句型荟萃：**

I think I will... 我觉得我会……

I'm sure I will... 我确信我会……

There will be... 将会有……

What...will be like...? ……将会是什么样？

...will be...in...years. 未来……年将会是……

**分层写作：**

基础层：根据语境，用所给词或短语的正确形式填空，使句意通顺。

| ask | homework | be | join | interest |
|---|---|---|---|---|

### My Ideal School Life

I am a student in Grade 8. We have five classes every day. I like all the lessons because they are very interesting and useful.

I hope our after-school activities will be rich and colorful. We can play many games after school every day. There will be many clubs in our school. I will join the clubs I am interested in, such as singing and English clubs. What's more, I also hope our homework will be not so much. I wish our teachers and classmates will be very helpful and kind. If you have a problem, you can ask the teachers and classmates for help.

This is my ideal school life. I hope my dream will come true some day.

提高层:根据括号内所给信息填空。

### My Ideal School Life

I am a student in Grade 8. We have five classes every day. I like all the lessons because they are very interesting and useful(因为它们非常有趣且有用).

I hope our after-school activities will be rich and colorful. We can play many games after school every day. There will be many clubs in our school(在我们学校将有很多社团). I will join the clubs I am interested in(我感兴趣的), such as singing and English clubs. What's more, I also hope our homework will be not so much(我也希望我们的作业不要太多). I wish our teachers and classmates will be very helpful and kind. If you have a problem, you can ask the teachers and classmates for help(你可以求助老师和同学).

This is my ideal school life. I hope my dream will come true some day.

发展层:根据指令完成任务。

### My Ideal School Life

I am a student in Grade 8. We have five classes every day. I like all the lessons because they are very interesting and useful.

I hope our after-school activities will be rich and colorful. ① We can play many games after school every day. There will be many clubs in our school. ② I will join the clubs I am interested in, such as singing and English clubs. What's more, I also hope our homework will be not so much. ③ I wish our teachers and classmates will be very helpful and kind. If you have a problem, you can ask the teachers and classmates for help.

This is my ideal school life. I hope my dream will come true some day.

1. 用"There is no doubt that…"句型改写①处画线句子。

There is no doubt that we can play many games after school every day

2. 将②处复合句改为简单句。

I will join the clubs. I am interested in these clubs

3. 将③处改为 who 引导的定语从句。

I wish I will have the teachers and classmates who are very helpful and kind.

## Unit 8 How do you make a banana milk shake?

### ☞ 话题分析

本单元的写作主题是"食物制作"。写作内容是描述一种食物的制作过程,包括所需材料,具体步骤、方法和注意事项等。写作时要使用祈使句及表示先后顺序的连接词,如 first、next、then、finally 等;一般现在时为主要时态。

**基本框架:**

引出主题:Do you know how to make…? I'd like to introduce the ways of making…

制作过程:First,… next,… then,… finally/in the end …

总结评价:Now,…is ready. It's time to enjoy it. It's really delicious!

### ☞ 典例剖析

今天你的朋友来家里做客,想尝尝你自己做的饺子。请你以"How to Make Dumplings"为题,向你的朋友介绍饺子的制作方法吧。

要求:80 个词左右,语言规范。不得出现真实的人名、校名等。

**写作点拨：**

时态：一般现在时

人称：第一人称；第二人称

体裁：说明文

**短语储备：**

knead the dough 揉面团

**句型荟萃：**

Don't forget to do… 别忘记做……

Remember to do… 记住要做……

**分层写作：**

基础层：根据语境，用所给词或短语的正确形式填空，使句意通顺。

| |
|---|
| help vegetable piece salt make then |

How to Make Dumplings

I'll make dumplings for you, so now let me tell you how to make dumplings. Here is a recipe for making dumplings. First, you should prepare some ingredients, such as meat and vegetables. Then, wash the vegetables and cut them up. Next, cut the meat into pieces and mix it with vegetables. If you have a machine to help you, don't forget to turn it on before you put the meat into it.

If the meat and vegetables are ready, you can mix them together and add some salt. For the following time you can knead the dough and remember to pour the flour into a pot. Finally, it's time for you to make dumplings. After a few minutes, we can enjoy delicious dumplings.

提高层：根据括号内所给信息填空。

How to Make Dumplings

I'll make dumplings for you, so now let me tell you how to make dumplings. Here is a recipe for making dumplings(这是做饺子的食谱). First, you should prepare some ingredients, such as meat and vegetables. Then, wash the vegetables and cut them up(洗菜并把菜切碎). Next, cut the meat into pieces and mix it with vegetables. If you have a machine to help you, don't forget to turn it on (别忘了把机器打开) before you put the meat into it.

If the meat and vegetables are ready, you can mix them together (把它们拌在一起) and add some salt. For the following time you can knead the dough and remember to pour the flour into a pot(记得把面倒进锅里). Finally, it's time for you to make dumplings. After a few minutes, we can enjoy delicious dumplings.

发展层:根据指令完成任务。

### How to Make Dumplings

I'll make dumplings for you, so now let me tell you how to make dumplings. ① Here is a recipe for making dumplings. First, you should prepare some ingredients, such as meat and vegetables. Then, wash the vegetables and cut them up. Next, cut the meat into pieces and mix it with vegetables. ②If you have a machine to help you, don't forget to turn it on before you put the meat into it.

If the meat and vegetables are ready, you can mix them together and add some salt. For the following time you can knead the dough and remember to pour the flour into a pot. Finally, it's time for you to make dumplings. After a few minutes, we can enjoy delicious dumplings.

③ ________

1. 将①处句子改为"做饺子,懂得食谱是很重要的。"(使用"It's+adj. +to do sth."句式)

It's important to know the recipe of making dumplings.

2. 将②处句子用 as long as 改写。

As long as you have a machine to help you, remember to turn it on before you put the meat into it.

3. 如果在文章结尾③处增加一句话,你会写什么呢?

I think we will have a good time together. (Answers may vary.)

## Unit 9 Can you come to my party?

### ☞ 话题分析

本单元的写作话题是"发出、接受或拒绝邀请"。向别人发出邀请时,语气应委婉,且带有一定的感情色彩。收到邀请但有事不能去或不想去因而要拒绝邀请时,也应该语气委婉、不失礼貌。邀请函的内容一般包括:聚会或活动的类型,举办的时间、地点,客人的着装,是否须带礼物,是否须答复,等等。回复邀请函时,若要拒绝邀请,一般先表达接受的意愿,再委婉地拒绝,接着说明理由,最后表示歉意以及祝福。

**基本框架:**

**邀请函**

Dear ________,

I'd like to ________. It will be ________. (*Beginning*: *what*+*when*+*where*)

During the party, you can ____________________. I would also like to ________________. (*Body*: *activities*, *preparations*)

I look forward to hearing from you. (*Ending*)

**接受邀请**

Thank you very much for inviting me. /I'm thankful for your invitation. /I'm glad to hear from you. (*Beginning*:表达感谢)

重复 when、where、who、how、what 等信息。(*Accepting an invitation*)

再次表达感谢。Thanks for inviting me once again. (*Ending*)

**拒绝邀请**

Thank you very much for inviting me. /I'm thankful for your invitation. /I'm glad to hear from you. (*Beginning*：表达感谢)

1. 拒绝。I'm sorry I can't come to.../I'm afraid I can't.

2. 理由。I'm very busy that day. I have to/must...

3. 提出帮助。

Though I can't come, I still would like to try my best to help you.

Please let me know if you need any help. (*Refusing an invitation*)

4. 再次表达感谢。Thanks for inviting me once again.

5. 美好祝福。I hope you can have a good time! (*Ending*)

## ☞ 典例剖析

假如你是黄敏，你的弟弟2024年高考考入清华大学，你特意邀请你的好友李文和姜轩来你家参加庆贺会。请你写一封邀请函，向李文和姜轩发出诚挚邀请。

内容要点：

1. 庆贺会于2024年8月15日在家举行；庆贺会结束后，大家一起坐黄河游艇(yacht)观赏黄河风情线。

2. 不用带任何礼物，父母在家备餐，快乐为主要宗旨。

3. 下周二之前回话。

要求：80个词左右；语言规范、观点合理。

**写作点拨：**

时态：一般将来时

人称：第一人称

体裁：应用文

**短语储备：**

serve food 提供食物

pursue happiness 追求快乐

make it 成功

**句型荟萃：**

Thanks for asking me to...感谢你邀请我……

Can you come to...? 你能来……吗？

I'd love to, but I have to... 我很想去，但不得不……

**分层写作：**

发展层：请补全写给李文和姜轩的邀请函。

Dear Li Wen and Jiang Xuan,

I would like to invite you to a celebration party for my brother to go to Tsinghua University. Because of my parents' joy, we decide to hold the celebration party at our house on August 15th, 2024 before he goes to Beijing.

You do not need to bring anything because we aim to pursue happiness. My parents are serving food and drinks from 5:30 p. m at home. After the meal, we will take a Yellow River Yacht to enjoy the Yellow River Custom Tourist Line. We can appreciate so much beauty, such as Zhongshan Iron Bridge, Baita Mountain, *Yellow River Mother* and so on.

Please reply by next Tuesday. I hope you can make it!

Huang Min

基础层：假如你是李文，你在2024年8月15日有空，可以参加黄敏弟弟的庆贺会，请你写一封信，表示接受黄敏的邀请。

Dear Huang Min,

Thank you very much for your invitation. It will be great pleasure for me to join (我很乐意参加) your brother's celebration party on August 15th. I will arrive at your home before 4:30 p. m. on that day. I look forward to meeting you(我期盼见到你) soon.

Thank you for thinking of me.

Yours,

Li Wen

提高层：假如你是姜轩，2024年8月15日那天，你正好要参加中学生羽毛球比赛，不能出席黄敏弟弟的庆贺会，请你写一封信，委婉拒绝黄敏的邀请。

Dear Huang Min,

Thanks for your invitation. I'm so sorry that I can't come to your brother's celebration party on August 15th. On that day, I have to join in the Badminton

Competition for Middle School Students. It's a pity that I can't come. It must be very fun! Wish you have a good time!

Yours,

Jiang Xuan

## Unit 10 If you go to the party, you'll have a great time!

### ☞ 话题分析

本单元的写作话题是"青少年在生活中遇到的困难及其引发的感受和事情的后果,并能针对问题提出建议"。学生需要准确使用 if 引导的条件状语从句来提出具体的问题,要特别注意主句及从句的时态问题,然后用情态动词 should 或 shouldn't 给别人提出建议。

**基本框架:**

第一段:引出主题。It's normal for…to… I have some advice for… Here is my advice.

第二段:给出建议。If you…, you'll… I think you should… You'd better… To be…, you should… It's best (not) to…

第三段:给予关怀。Follow the advice/suggestions, and you will… I'm sure you will… I really hope you can solve the problems and…

### ☞ 典例剖析

青少年在成长过程中难免会遇到一些困惑。下表是 Jim 的一些烦恼。假设你是 Jim 的朋友 Alice,请你根据下表内容,给 Jim 写一封信,为他提出合理的建议。

| Problems | Advice |
|---|---|
| has lots of homework and can't do what he likes | … |
| is a little heavy and worried about his health | … |
| … | … |

要求:1. 语句通顺、符合逻辑,可适当发挥;

2. 70 个词左右。

**写作点拨:**

时态:一般现在时

人称:第一人称;第二人称

体裁:应用文

**分层写作:**

基础层:根据语境,用所给词或短语的正确形式填空,使句意通顺。

| find that vegetable cut do talk to normal little |
|---|

Dear Jim,

I'm sorry to hear that you have some problems in your life.

You said that you have so much homework that you have no time to do what you like. Why don't you talk to your teachers? If you do, they will know more about their students' problems and give you less homework.

You are also worried about your health. I think doing sports can help you a lot. What's more, you should eat more fruit and vegetables.

Problems are normal in life. When you have one, the first step is to find someone to talk to. Sharing a problem is like cutting it in half.

Hope you can be better soon.

Yours,

Alice

提高层:根据括号内所给信息填空。

Dear Jim,

I'm sorry to hear that you have some problems in your life.

You said that you have so much homework that you have no time to do(你没时间做) what you like. Why don't you talk to your teachers? If you do, they will know more about their students' problems and give you less homework.

You are also worried about(也为……担心) your health. I think doing sports can help you a lot. What's more, you should eat more fruit and vegetables(你应该多吃水果和蔬菜).

Problems are normal in life. When you have one, the first step is to find someone to talk to（找人交流）. Sharing a problem is like cutting it in half.

Hope you can be better soon.

Yours,

Alice

发展层：根据指令完成任务。

Dear Jim,

I'm sorry to hear that you have some problems in your life.

You said that ① you have so much homework that you have no time to do what you like. ② Why don't you talk to your teachers? If you do, they will know more about their students' problems and give you less homework.

You are also worried about your health. I think doing sports can help you a lot. What's more, ③ you should eat more fruit and vegetables.

Problems are normal in life. When you have one, ④ the first step is to find someone to talk to. Sharing a problem is like cutting it in half.

Hope you can be better soon.

Yours,

Alice

1. 将①处句子改为"too…to…"结构，保持句意不变。

your homework is too much for you to have time to do what you like

2. 用"Why not…?"改写②处句子。

Why not talk to your teachers?

3. 将③处内容用强调句型改写，强调宾语。

it is more fruit and vegetables that you should eat

4. 将④处画线句子改写为表语从句。

the first step is that you should find someone to talk to

## 第四节　八年级下册

经过了八年级上册的写作训练，根据学生的实际情况，教师可将分层练习模式恢复到七年级的模式,同时增加“师生互动:修辞润色”环节,以便学生掌握修辞润色的方法,进一步提高学生的写作技能。

## Unit 1 What's the matter?

### ☞ 话题分析

本单元以“健康与急救”为话题,要求学生针对健康问题或意外事故提出建议。写作时,学生需要准确描述某一健康或意外问题,并能运用情态动词should/shouldn't给出适当的建议,最后表示祝愿,希望对方早日康复。体裁以应用文、记叙文、说明文为主,时态可能涉及一般现在时、一般过去时和一般将来时,多采用第二人称。

### ☞ 素材积累

**【单词】**

身体部位:foot 脚;足 stomach 胃;腹部 throat 咽喉;喉咙 knee 膝盖;膝关节

健康相关:stomachache 胃痛;肚子痛 fever 发烧 cough 咳嗽 ache 疼痛;隐痛 pain 疼痛 well 健康;身体好

急救相关:blood 血 death 死;死亡 hurt (使)疼痛,受伤 hit (用手或器具)击,打

**【短语】**

have a fever 发烧

have a sore throat 喉咙痛

have a toothache 牙痛

have a stomachache 胃痛;肚子痛

take one's temperature 量某人的体温

go to a doctor 去看医生

get an X-ray 拍个 X 光片

lie down and rest 躺下休息

cut off 切断；切掉

give up 放弃

run out of 用完，耗尽

in excellent condition 健康状况很好

【句型】

What's the matter with you? 你怎么了？

You should take your temperature. 你应该量体温。

You should drink some hot water with honey. 你应该喝一些加蜂蜜的热水。

You need to take breaks away from the computer. 你需要离开电脑、休息一下。

## ☞ 典例剖析

> 你的好朋友 Lisa 今天早上感觉不舒服，头痛、脖子动弹不得。她量了体温，发现自己发高烧了。请你根据以下要点，介绍一下 Lisa 的情况，给出你对她的建议，并希望她早日康复。
>
> 要点：1. 描述 Lisa 的病情；2. 分析原因；3. 给出建议。
>
> 要求：1. 内容包括提示中的所有写作要点；
>
> 2. 条理清楚，行文连贯，可适当发挥；
>
> 3. 文中不能出现真实的人名和地名等信息；
>
> 4. 词数不少于 80 个。

**第一步：读题审题**

审
- 主题：健康与急救
- 体裁：记叙文
- 人称：第三人称
- 时态：一般现在时；一般过去时；一般将来时

**第二步：写作提纲**

开篇点题：引出好朋友的问题。my good friend Lisa has trouble with/in doing sth.

正文部分:分析病因并提出建议。I know she likes playing computer games, maybe she…I think she should…she needs to…she shouldn't…either

结尾部分:对好朋友的美好祝愿。I think she will…

**第三步:分层写作**

基础层:仿写句子

take a break/take breaks 休息一下

**【例句】**你需要离开电脑、休息一下。

You need to take breaks away from the computer.

**【仿写】**我们去树下休息一下吧。

Let's take a break under the tree.

lie down 躺下

**【例句】**我认为你应该躺下休息。I think you should lie down and rest.

**【仿写】**我太累了,需要躺下休息一会儿。

I'm too tired and need to lie down and rest.

提高层:扩写句子

**【例句】**She has a very sore throat.(扩写原因"因为她得了感冒")

→She has a very sore throat because she got a cold.

**【练习】**I have a headache and my neck hurts.(扩写原因"因为我发高烧")

→I have a headache and my neck hurts because I had a high fever.

发展层:连句成章

My good friend Lisa didn't feel well this morning. She had a headache and she couldn't move her neck. She took her temperature by herself and found that she had a high fever.

I know she likes playing computer games. Maybe she spent lots of time playing computer games last night and sat in the same way for too long without moving. So I think she should take breaks away from the computer. She needs to lie down and rest. She shouldn't use the computer for a long time. Exercise can help us build up our bodies. So she should try to exercise more often.

I think she will feel well soon after a good rest.

师生互动:修辞润色

My good friend Lisa didn't feel well this morning. What I feel like telling everyone is that (加上引入语,原句变为从句,使句子更高级) she had a headache and she couldn't move her neck. She took her temperature by herself and found that she had a high fever.

I know she likes playing computer games. Maybe it is last night that (使用强调句来强调时间) she spent lots of time playing computer games and sat in the same way for too long without moving. So I think she should take breaks away from the computer. She needs to lie down and rest. She shouldn't use the computer for a long time. It' s well-known that(加上常用表达,令 it 做形式主语,使句子更高级) exercise can help us build up our bodies. So she should try to exercise more often.

I think she will feel well soon after a good rest.

## Unit 2 I'll help to clean up the city parks.

### ☞ 话题分析

本单元谈论的话题是"志愿者活动"。作文通常采用日记、通知、书信等形式,写作时要能够清楚地把提示性文字表达出来:首先,点明题意,主要介绍志愿者的活动安排;然后,陈述活动的具体内容;最后,表达自己对这次活动的期待或感受。

**基本框架:**

第一段:介绍自己。(name, age, from…)

I think it's a good chance for me to be a volunteer.

第二段:怎样做志愿工作。

1. 种类:I would like to …/I'm interested in …

2. 兴趣和爱好:I'm good at…/In my free time, I like to…, so I think I'd be good at…

3. 原因：I want to help out as a volunteer in your people's home… because…

第三段：总结。

Volunteering is great. I think I will be a good volunteer.

## ☞ 素材积累

**【单词】**

volunteer 志愿者　raise 筹集　understand 理解　kindness 仁慈　train 训练　repair/fix up 修理

**【短语】**

hope to do sth. 希望做某事

volunteer to do sth. 志愿做某事

be interested in sth. 对某事/物感兴趣

clean up 打扫干净

cheer up 振作起来

give away 捐赠；赠送

**【句型】**

I'll help to clean up the city parks. 我会帮忙打扫城市公园。

The boys could give out food at the food bank. 男孩们可以在"食物银行"(食物赈济处)分发食物。

We could put up signs. 我们可以贴告示。

I get such a strong feeling of satisfaction. 我有一种强烈的满足感。

Being a volunteer is really great. 做志愿者真好。

I volunteer to do something. 我自愿做些事。

**【佳句集锦】**

It is better to give than to take. 施予比索取更好。

Helping others is a virtue. 助人为乐是一种美德。

Roses given, fragrance in hand. 赠人玫瑰，手有余香。

If someone is in trouble, everyone will help. 一方有难，八方支援。

## ☞ 典例剖析

假如你是李明,在本周班会上,你将代表英语老师用英语通知同学们参加一次养老院的公益活动。

要点:

1. 星期天早上8:30在校门口集合,乘公共汽车前往养老院;
2. 给老人们赠送班级礼物;
3. 打扫卫生,整理房间;
4. 唱歌、跳舞、讲故事、聊天,给老人们带去快乐;
5. 活动很有意义,希望同学们积极参加;
6. 补充一到两点你对本次活动的看法。

**第一步:读题审题**

审{
体裁:应用文
主题:志愿与奉献
人称:第一人称
时态:一般现在时;一般将来时

**第二步:写作提纲**

第一段:总述,引起下文。We will pay a visit to the old people's home this Sunday.

第二段:描述具体的活动。We will do some cleaning and tidy the rooms. We will have many activities, such as singing, dancing and telling stories…

第三段:阐述对该活动的看法。take an active part; learn to care for the old…

**第三步:分层写作**

基础层:仿写句子

cheer sb. up 鼓舞某人

【例句】这个女孩可以拜访医院里生病的孩子们以鼓舞他们。

The girl could visit the sick kids in the hospital to cheer them up.

【仿写】我们试图让母亲振作起来。

We tried our best to cheer our mom up.

fix up 修理

【例句】艾伦在修理自己的自行车。

Alan is fixing up his own bike.

【仿写】吉米正在修理破损的自行车部件，如轮子。

Jimmy is fixing up the broken bike parts, such as wheels.

Thank you for doing sth. 因某事而感谢你

【例句】感谢您给我的无私帮助。

Thank you for giving me selfless help.

【仿写】我想谢谢你资助“动物帮手”。

I'd like to thank you for supporting the "animal-helper".

提高层：扩写句子

【例句】After that we will have many activities.（扩写具体活动“唱歌、跳舞、讲故事、聊天，来让老人振作起来”）

→After that we will have many activities, such as singing, dancing, telling stories and chatting to cheer up the old.

【练习】I hope all of us can take an active part.（扩写原因“因为通过有意义的活动，我们能够学会照顾老人”）

→I hope all of us can take an active part because we can learn to care for the old through the meaningful activities.

发展层：连句成章

Fellow Students,

We will pay a visit to the old people's home this Sunday. We'll have to meet at the school gate at 8:30 on Sunday morning and then go there by bus. There we will do some cleaning and tidy the rooms. After that we will have many activities, such as singing, dancing, telling stories and chatting to cheer up the old. Before we leave, we'll give our presents to them.

I hope all of us can take an active part. Through the meaningful activities, we can learn to care for the old.

师生互动：修辞润色

Fellow Students,

We will pay a visit to the old people's home this Sunday. It's at the school gate that(强调地点状语) we'll have to meet at 8:30 on Sunday morning and then go there by bus. There we will do some cleaning and tidy the rooms. After that we will have many activities, such as singing, dancing, telling stories and chatting to cheer up the old. Before we leave, we'll give our presents to them.

I hope all of us can take an active part. Only by joining in the meaningful activities can we(only by 后接部分倒装) learn to care for the old.

## Unit 3 Could you please clean your room?

### ☞ 话题分析

本单元的话题是"做家务",需要学生以议论文的形式表达自己对做家务的观点和看法,进一步可以延伸为对一些现象、热点等发表观点和看法,并能用一些论据来支撑自己的观点。学生在写作时既要详细描述做家务的内容,还要描述自己的感受、表达自己的观点和看法。写作时也可提到他人的观点和看法,然后表达自己的态度,并说明原因。

### ☞ 素材积累

【单词】

家务相关:rubbish 垃圾 sweep 打扫 chore 家庭杂务 throw 扔 fold 折叠 shirt 衬衫 waste 浪费 floor 地板 drop 落下 mess 杂乱

【短语】

do the dishes 洗碗

clean up 打扫

take out the trash/rubbish 倒垃圾

fold your clothes 叠衣服

sweep the floor 扫地

make your bed 铺床

clean the living room 打扫客厅

go out for a dinner 外出吃饭

stay out late 在外边待到很晚

clean the room 打扫房间

【句型】

Could you please sweep the floor? 你能扫一下地吗?

I have to do some housework. 我必须做些家务。

It's good for students to do housework. 做家务对学生有好处。

I finally understand that we need to share the housework to have a clean and comfortable home. 我最终明白我们需要分担家务来拥有一个干净且舒适的家。

I don't understand why some parents make their kids help with housework and chores at home. 我不明白为什么一些家长让他们的孩子在家帮忙做家务。

There is no need for them to do housework. 没有必要让他们做家务。

It's important for children to learn how to do chores and help their parents with housework. 对孩子们来说,学着做家务和帮助他们的父母做家务是很重要的。

The earlier kids learn to be independent, the better it is for their future. 孩子们越早学会独立,对他们的未来就越好。

## ☞ 典例剖析

在昨天的班会课上,同学们就中学生是否应该做家务进行了激烈的讨论。有人认为中学生应该做家务,有人认为中学生没必要做家务。请你写一篇短文,说明你支持哪一个观点并阐述原因。

要点:1. 你对于做家务的观点;

2. 你持这种观点的原因;

3. 总结。

要求:1. 内容包括提示中所有的写作要点;

2. 条理清楚,有理有据,行文连贯,可适当发挥;

3. 文中不能出现真实的人名和地名等信息;

4. 词数不少于 80 个。

**第一步:读题审题**

审
- 体裁:议论文
- 主题:中学生是否该做家务
- 人称:第一人称;第三人称
- 时态:一般现在时

**第二步:写作提纲**

第一段:引出话题,就"中学生是否应当承担家务"这一问题阐明自己的观点。It's very important for us to be independent.

第二段:展开论述。First… Second… Third… Finally…

第三段:总结呼应。I think if we keep on doing these, we'll become more and more independent.

**第三步:分层写作**

基础层:仿写句子

do one's part in doing sth. 尽某人一份力做某事

【例句】孩子们应该知道,每个人都应该为保持房间的干净与整洁尽一份力。

Children should know that everyone should do their part in keeping the room clean and tidy.

【仿写】保护环境,人人有责。

Every one should do his part in protecting the environment.

a waste of time 浪费时间

【例句】做家务浪费他们的时间。Housework is a waste of their time.

【仿写】下雨的时候给花浇水就是在浪费时间。

It's a waste of time to water flowers when it's raining.

提高层:扩写句子

【例句】Others believe there is no need for middle school students to do the housework.(扩写原因"因为他们有来自学校的太多的压力并且没时间做家务")

→Others believe there is no need for middle school students to do the housework because they have too much stress from school and they have no time to do chores.

【练习】Some students think it's necessary for children to do chores.（扩写原因"因为它帮助学生发展他们的独立性以及理解公平的含义"）

→Some students think it's necessary for children to do chores because it helps students to develop their independence and understand the idea of fairness.

发展层：连句成章

Yesterday, we had a heated discussion about whether middle school students should do housework in the class meeting. Some students think it's necessary. However, others believe that there is no need for them to do that.

In my opinion, doing housework is good. First, parents are often tired after work. If we can help them with housework, they will feel much better. Second, we can't always depend on others. For example, we should make the beds and clean the rooms. So it's a good way to develop our independence. It can make us understand our parents more. Third, I think that students should do chores at home because it is not enough to just study hard and do well at school.

In a word, I believe that middle school students should do some housework because it's good for both students and parents.

师生互动：修辞润色

Yesterday, we had a heated discussion about whether middle school students should do housework in the class meeting. Some students think it's necessary. However, others believe that it's not essential for them to do that("there is no need for them to do that"的同义句转换).

In my opinion, doing housework is good. First, parents are often tired after work. If we can help them with housework, they will feel much better. Second, we can't always depend on others. For example, we should make the beds and clean the rooms. So it's a good way to develop our independence. It can make us understand our parents more. Third, I think that students should do whatever they can to do chores (do whatever sb. can to do 的应用，表示"尽力而为") at home because it is not enough to just study hard and do well at school.

In a word, I believe that middle school students should do some housework because it's good for both students and parents.

## Unit 4 Why don't you talk to your parents?

### ☞ 话题分析

本单元的话题是"学习生活中的问题",要求学生能简单描述青少年在学习生活中普遍存在的问题,进而对这些问题提出合理的建议,并阐述理由。写作体裁以议论文为主,时态可能涉及一般现在时,人称多采用第一、二、三人称。

### ☞ 素材积累

【单词】

问题:worry 烦心事　stress 压力　difficulty 困难　trouble 麻烦　pressure 压力　problem 问题

活动:after-school activity 课外活动　schoolwork 学校作业　exercise 锻炼　compete 竞争　relax 放松

建议:opinion 意见　suggest 建议　advise 建议

【短语】

be angry with sb. 对某人生气

get into a fight with sb. 与某人打架(争吵)

get on well with classmates 与同学友好相处

compete with classmates 与同学竞争

refuse to let me watch TV 拒绝让我看电视

hang out with friends 与朋友闲逛

play sports or exercise 做运动或进行锻炼

push sb. too hard 把某人逼得太紧

【句型】

I don't have any time to do things I like. 我没有任何时间去做我喜欢的事情。

Don't get into a fight with your classmates. 不要与同学打架。

He spent too much time on schoolwork. 他在学校作业上花了太多时间。

Our parents want us to be successful. 我们的父母想要我们取得成功。

She thinks her parents push her too hard. 她觉得她的父母把她逼得太紧了。

## ☞ 典例剖析

Tina 的朋友 Tom 要过生日,别人准备的礼物都很贵重,可她却没有足够的钱给 Tom 买昂贵的礼物。她写信给 Jack 以得到一些建议。假如你是 Jack,请你根据提示给 Tina 写一封回信,为她提供一些合理的建议。

提示:1. 礼物并不一定是贵的就好;

2. 没必要为此伤心;

3. 友谊不是金钱能衡量的;

4. 可以动手自制贺卡。

要求:1. 内容须包括提示中所有的写作要点;

2. 条理清楚,行文连贯,可适当发挥;

3. 文中不能出现真实的人名和地名等信息;

4. 词数不少于 80 个。

**第一步:读题审题**

审
- 体裁:议论文
- 主题:困难与麻烦
- 人称:第二人称;第三人称
- 时态:一般现在时

**第二步:写作提纲**

第一段:开头问候并点明问题。I'm glad to receive your letter. You asked me…(问题)

第二段:具体阐述写信意图与建议。Here's some advice for you. Firstly, I think it's important to…(建议一) Secondly, …(建议二) is necessary. What's more, …(建议三)

第三段:表达希望。I'm looking forward to…(期望)

**第三步:分层写作**

基础层:仿写句子

push sb. too hard 逼某人太紧

【例句】Linda 认为一些父母把他们的孩子逼太紧了。

Linda thinks some parents push their kids too much.

【仿写】照顾好自己,不要逼自己太紧。

Take care of yourself and don't push yourself too hard.

compare A with B 把 A 与 B 做比较

【例句】他们总是拿自己的孩子与其他孩子做比较。

They always compare their children with other children.

【仿写】不要总是拿自己与别人做比较。

Don't always compare yourself with others.

提高层:扩写句子

【例句】Children already have lots of pressure from school（扩写结果"所以他们需要时间来休息并花一些时间在他们的爱好上"）

→Children already have lots of pressure from school. So they need time to relax and spend some time on their hobbies.

【练习】I think children can make better use of weekends.（扩写事件"而不是参加所有种类的课外班"）

→I think children can make better use of weekends instead of taking all kinds of after-school classes.

发展层:连句成章

Dear Tina,

Glad to hear from you, but I'm sorry to hear that you are so worried. In my opinion, gifts are just something to show your love. Friendship can't be measured by money.

I don't think you need to buy an expensive gift. It will cost too much money. And if you don't have too much money, you have to ask your parents for it. It is a good idea to buy some flowers and make a beautiful birthday card by yourself. That's be enough to make your friend happy.

How about my advice?

Yours,

Jack

师生互动:修辞润色

Dear Tina,

Glad to hear from you, but I'm sorry to hear that you are so worried. In my opinion, gifts are just something to show your love. As is known to all(加上常见的引入语"众所周知"), friendship can't be measured by money.

I don't think you need to buy an expensive gift. It will cost too much money. And unless you have too much money("if you don't have too much money"的同义句,unless=if...not...), you have to ask your parents for it. It is a good idea to buy some flowers and make a beautiful birthday card by yourself. That's be enough to make your friend happy.

How about my advice?

Yours,

Jack

## Unit 5 What were you doing when the rainstorm came?

### ☞ 话题分析

本单元的话题是"谈论过去正在发生的事情",要求学生能够对过去正在发生的事情进行描述。在写作时,学生要围绕中心,清晰地叙述事件发生的时间、地点、人物、经过,以及事件发生时人物的所做所悟。体裁以记叙文为主,时态可能涉及一般过去时和过去进行时,人称常采用第一人称或第三人称。

### ☞ 素材积累

【单词】

suddenly 突然地 strange 陌生的 report 报道 beat 敲击 fall 进入某种状态 rise 升起;上涨 realize 意识到 completely 完全地 recently 最近 truth 真相 shocked 感到震惊的 fallen 倒塌的

【短语】

begin/come to realize... 开始意识到……

... was/were doing... when... 当……时,……正在……

so… that… 如此……以至于……

go off 发出响声

die down 逐渐减弱

make one's way to… 努力向……前进

take down 拆除

in silence 沉默，无声

in a mess 一团糟

have meaning to… 对……有意义

【句型】

When he woke up, the sun was rising. 当他醒来时，太阳正在升起。

He went out with his family and found the neighborhood in a mess. 他和家人来到外面，发现街区凌乱不堪。

My parents were completely shocked. 我的父母被完全震惊了。

I didn't believe him at first. 起初，我并不相信他。

I was so scared that I could hardly think clearly after that. 在那之后，我感到非常恐惧，以至于我无法清晰地思考。

It was hard to have fun with a serious storm happening outside. 外面暴风雨肆虐，我们很难开心起来。

## ☞ 典例剖析

请你以"An Unforgettable Thing"为题，简要描述一件让你印象深刻的事情，并谈谈你从这件事中所获得的启示。要点如下：

①What was the event?

②When did it happen?

③Where did it happen?

④What were you doing?

⑤What were your friends doing?

⑥Why was it important?

要求：1. 内容齐全，行文连贯；

2. 80 个词左右。

**第一步:读题审题**

审
- 体裁:记叙文
- 主题:难忘的事
- 人称:第一人称
- 时态:一般现在时;一般过去时;过去进行时

**第二步:写作提纲**

第一段:Introduction. Write about the event(when and where it happened)

第二段:Details of the event. Write about what you and some of your friends were doing when this event happened.

第三段:Feelings or reasons. Write why this event was important.

**第三步:分层写作**

基础层:仿写句子

was/were doing sth.(过去某一时刻)正在做某事

**【例句】**听到此消息时,我们正在厨房吃晚饭。

We were eating the dinner in the kitchen when we heard the news.

**【仿写】**当这件事情发生时,我正跑得很快。

I was running fast when it happened.

although/though... 虽然……

**【例句】**虽然暴风雨把许多东西弄得七零八落,但是它让我们的家庭和邻里关系更加紧密。

Although the storm broke many things apart, it brought families and neighbors closer together.

**【仿写】**虽然我很累,但我仍然坚持跑着。

Though/although I was very tired, I was still keeping on running.

提高层:扩写句子

**【例句】**This event is very important to me.(扩写原因"因为意识到友谊的重要性")

→This event is very important to me because I realize how important the friendship is!

【练习】I was running very fast.(扩写目的“要拿一等奖”)

→I was running very fast to get the first prize.

发展层:连句成章

### An Unforgettable Thing

An important event that I remember well is that I broke my leg. It happened on the school sports day last year on the playground.

When this event happened, I was running very fast to get the first prize. My friends were cheering me on. Although I was very tired, I was still keeping on running. With the last ten meters, suddenly, I fell down and broke my leg. It really hurt and I couldn't stop crying. My friends ran towards me and took me to the hospital. After that, my friends cared about me with my schoolwork and my health. I recovered soon and I came back to school.

This event is very important to me because I realize how important the friendship is!

师生互动:修辞润色

### An Unforgettable Thing

An important event that I remember well is that I broke my leg. It happened on the school sports day last year on the playground.

When this event happened, I was running very fast to get the first prize. My friends were cheering me on. Very tired as I was(“Although I was very tired”的同义句转换,用 as 引起部分倒装), I was still keeping on running. With the last ten meters, suddenly, I fell down and broke my leg. It really hurt and I couldn't stop crying. My friends who took me to the hospital ran towards me(将原句改为定语从句). After that, my friends cared about me with my schoolwork and my health. I recovered soon and I came back to school.

This event is very important to me because I realize how important the friendship is!

# Unit 6 An old man tried to move the mountains.

## ☞ 话题分析

本单元的话题是“讲故事”，要求学生能够简单讲述民间传说与童话故事。写作时，学生要用所学的简单语言及恰当时态讲述一个故事，并能正确运用 unless、as soon as、so…that 等表达以增强故事的逻辑性和连贯性，在作文结尾点明故事的寓意。体裁以记叙文为主，时态多用一般过去时，人称多采用第三人称。

## ☞ 素材积累

**【单词】**

人物：prince/princess 王子/公主 stepmother/stepsister 继母/继姐妹 emperor 皇帝 couple 夫妻；两人；两件事物

单词：weak 虚弱的；无力的 remind 提醒；使想起 hide 藏；隐蔽；躲避 excite 使激动；使兴奋 bright 明亮的；光亮地 brave 勇敢的；无畏的

**【短语】**

神话故事：

*Hou Yi Shoots the Suns*《后羿射日》

*Nü Wa Repairs the Sky*《女娲补天》

*Yu Gong Moves the Mountains*《愚公移山》

*Journey to the West*《西游记》

*Magic Brush Ma Liang*《神笔马良》

*Chang'e Flies to the Moon*《嫦娥奔月》

其他短语：

work on doing sth. 致力于做某事

as soon as 一……就……

continue to do sth. 继续做某事

make sb. happy 使某人开心

keep on doing sth. 坚持做某事

give up doing sth. 放弃做某事

get married 结婚

be able to do sth. 能/会做某事

【句型】

So what do you think of the story of Yu Gong? 你觉得愚公的故事怎么样?

It doesn't seem possible to move a mountain. 移走一座山看起来不太可能。

But unless he can hide his tail, he cannot turn himself into a man. 但是除非他能把尾巴藏起来,否则他就不能变成人。

Don't eat it until you get to the forest. 你们到达森林之后才能吃。

## ☞ 典例剖析

《后羿射日》是一个古老的神话传说。请根据提示写一篇 80 个词左右的短文,简单介绍一下这个故事。

提示:

1. 从前,天上只有一个太阳,人们生活得很幸福。

2. 突然有一天,天上出现了十个太阳。天气是如此炎热以至于庄稼干枯、动物死亡。人们生活得很是艰难。

3. 有一位年轻人叫后羿。他擅长射箭。于是,人们就请求他把多余的九个太阳射下来。

4. 后羿登上海边的一座高山,射掉了九个太阳。

5. 人们非常感谢后羿。后来他娶了嫦娥,过上了幸福的生活。

要求:1. 条理清楚,行文连贯,可适当发挥;

2. 词数不少于 80 个。

**第一步:读题审题**

审
- 主题:讲故事
- 体裁:记叙文
- 人称:第三人称
- 时态:一般过去时

**第二步:写作提纲**

第一段:开头。开篇点题,介绍后羿射日的原因。

第二段:正文。具体叙述后羿射日的经过。

第三段:结尾。最后,后羿过着幸福的生活。

**第三步:分层写作**

基础层:仿写句子

so… that… 如此……以至于……

【例句】他是如此年老体弱以至于他无法移走大山 。

He was so old and weak that he couldn't move the mountains.

【仿写】天气是如此之热以至于庄稼都死了。

It's so hot that the crop all died.

as soon as 一……就……

【例句】那个人刚一说完,愚公就说他死后他的家人可以继续移山。

As soon as the man finished talking, Yu Gong said that his family could continue to move the mountains after he died.

【仿写】Jimmy 一到学校就开始读书。

Jimmy started to read books as soon as he arrived at school.

提高层:扩写句子

【例句】He is a little boy. (扩写细节"八岁""名叫 Bob""喜欢画画"等)

→He is an eight-year-old little boy called Bob. He likes drawing and often draws pictures in the park.

【练习】He decided to help mom. (扩写具体事件"做家务")

→ He decided to help mom with housework.

发展层:连句成章

### Hou Yi Shoots the Suns

Once upon a time, there was a sun in the sky and people had a happy life. But one day ten suns appeared in the sky. The weather was so hot that all the crops and many animals died. Unless there was only a sun, people couldn't have a happy life. A young man called Hou Yi was very good at shooting. He was so kind and brave that he decided to help people to shoot down nine suns. So he climbed the high mountain beside the sea. He had a lot of difficulties and tried his best to shoot nine suns. As soon as there was only a sun in the sky, people felt cooler and became very glad at once. At last, Hou Yi married Chang'e and they lived happily.

This story reminds us that you can never know what's possible unless you try to make it happen.

师生互动:修辞润色

### Hou Yi Shoots the Suns

Once upon a time, there was a sun in the sky and people had a happy life. But one day ten suns appeared in the sky. So hot was the weather(将 so hot 提前,引起部分倒装,改变句子结构) that all the crops and many animals died. Unless there was only a sun, people couldn't have a happy life.

A young man who is called Hou Yi (过去分词改为定语从句) was very good at shooting. He was so kind and brave that he decided to help people to shoot down nine suns. So he climbed the high mountain beside the sea. He had a lot of difficulties and tried his best to shoot nine suns. People felt cooler and became very glad at once the moment there was only a sun in the sky[将从句"as soon as there was only a sun in the sky"与主句改用 the moment(that)合并]. At last, Hou Yi married Chang'e and they lived happily.

This story reminds us that you can never know what's possible unless you try to make it happen.

## Unit 7 What's the highest mountain in the world?

### ☞ 话题分析

本单元的话题是"保护大自然",要求学生针对保护动物和自然资源提出具体措施或建议。写作时,学生要能根据所给信息或图片描述自然景观或野生动物的相关情况,并能运用情态动词 should/shouldn't、could 等给出适当的建议,最后表达祝愿或号召大家行动起来。体裁以应用文、记叙文、说明文为主,时态可能涉及一般现在时、一般过去时和一般将来时,人称多采用第一人称和第三人称。

## ☞ 素材积累

【单词】

位置与组成:wide 宽的;宽阔的 square 正方形;正方形的 huge 巨大的 the Nansha Islands 南沙群岛 condition 条件;状况

自然资源:resource 资源 be in danger 处于危险之中 rich 丰富的

自然景观:scenery 景色 nature 自然 environment 环境 attraction 有吸引力的人或事物

【短语】

as far as I know 据我所知

as you can see… 正如你所看见的……

as big as… 和……一样大

mineral resources 矿产资源

run along 跨越

be made up 由……组成

one of the most popular places 最受欢迎的地方之一

take in air 呼吸空气

protect…from… 保护……免受……伤害

be located in 位于;坐落于

even though/if 即使;虽然

in the face of 面对(问题、困难等)

【句型】

As is known to all, … are in danger now. 众所周知,……现在正处于危险之中。

…is/are one of the endangered animals. ……是濒危动物之一。

The number of … is getting smaller and smaller. ……的数量正变得越来越小。

… are in danger because … ……正处于危险之中,因为……

Humans cut down … and pollute … 人类砍倒……并且污染……

They don't have enough … to …, so … 他/她/它们没有足够的……来……,

所以……

What's worse, humans kill/catch ... for ... 更糟糕的是,人类杀死/捕获……来……

We should protect ... from ... 我们应该保护……免受……

I think people should/shouldn't ... 我认为人们应该/不应该……

It's time for us to protect ... 是我们保护……的时候了。

It's our duty to protect ... 保护……是我们的责任。

We should try our best to tell people the importance of ... 我们应该尽最大努力来告诉人们……的重要性。

We must take measures to ... 我们必须采取措施来……

We all hope that in the future ... 我们都希望未来……

## ☞ 典例剖析

请以"Saving Wild Tigers"为题,为某中学生英语报写一篇 80 个词左右的征文稿,内容要点如下:

(1)老虎是人们在动物园里最喜欢观看的动物之一;

(2)现在世界上仅存大约 4 000 只野生老虎;

(3)老虎处境危险的原因;

(4)保护老虎的建议。

注意:不可逐字逐句翻译,可以根据情况适度发挥。

**第一步:读题审题**

审:
- 体裁:应用文
- 主题:动物保护
- 人称:第三人称
- 时态:一般现在时

**第二步:写作提纲**

第一段:引入话题。I'm glad/delighted/happy/desirous to tell…about… which are ... They live in ... They eat ... They can ... As is known to all, ... are in danger now.

第二段:正文,说明原因。Some kinds of ... are in danger because ...What's worse, …

第三段:结尾,提出建议。We should protect… from… I think people should/shouldn't…

**第三步:分层写作**

基础层:仿写句子

as is known to all 众所周知

【例句】众所周知,成年大熊猫每天花超过12小时吃大约10公斤重的竹子。

As is known to all that adult pandas spend more than 12 hours a day eating about 10 kilos of bamboos.

【仿写】众所周知,黄河是中国第二条最长的河。

As is known to all, the Yellow River is the second longest river in China.

in danger 处境危险

【例句】有些动物处境极度危险。Some animals are in great danger.

【仿写】老虎也是处境危险的动物之一。

Tigers are also one of the animals in danger.

提高层:扩写句子

【例句】Tigers are one of the animals.(扩写细节"人们喜欢在动物园里看的动物")

→Tigers are one of the animals that people love to see in the zoo.

【练习】There are only 4 000 wild tigers.(扩写地点状语"在世界上")

→There are only 4 000 wild tigers that live in the world.

发展层:连句成章

## Saving Wild Tigers

As is known to all, tigers are one of the animals that people like to see most in the zoo. One surprising fact is that there are only 4 000 wild tigers in the world. Some kinds of tigers are in danger because humans catch them for fur, meat and bone, and use tiger parts to make things like medicine, food and decorations. What's worse, the environment the tigers live in is becoming more and more serious. Therefore, we should protect tigers from being killed by making rules on tigers protection and by not putting any polluted food in the environment that they live in. Actually, I think people should learn more about tigers.

师生互动:修辞润色

### Saving Wild Tigers

As is known to all, it is in the zoo that (强调地点状语) tigers are one of the animals that people like to see most. One surprising fact is that there are only 4 000 wild tigers in the world. Some kinds of tigers are in danger because humans catch them for fur, meat and bone, and use tiger parts to make things like medicine, food and decorations. What's worse, there is no doubt that (增加同位语从句,保持原句意思不变,增加句子结构的可读性) the environment the tigers live in is becoming more and more serious. Therefore, we should protect tigers from being killed by making rules on tigers protection and by not putting any polluted food in the environment that they live in. Actually, I think people should learn more about tigers.

## Unit 8 Have you read *Treasure Island* yet?

### ☞ 话题分析

本单元的话题是"文学和音乐",和该话题有关的书面表达通常是学生较为熟悉的内容,比如介绍或谈论一个歌手或作家。写作时,学生要用一般现在时和现在完成时,可先介绍想写的人,然后具体谈谈他/她的相关情况或喜欢他/她的原因,最后可表达自己的感受或感想等。文章要层次分明、感情真挚。

### ☞ 素材积累

**【单词】**

fiction 小说 science fiction 科幻小说 classic 经典作品;名著 pop 流行音乐 rock 摇滚乐 fan 迷;狂热爱好者(名词) country music 乡村音乐 record 唱片(名词);记录(动词) introduce 介绍 success 成功

【短语】

put down 放下

give up 放弃

be interested in... 对……感兴趣

can't wait to do sth. 迫不及待做某事

belong to 属于;归……所有

(be) full of energy 充满能量

used to do sth. 过去常常做某事

come to realize 逐渐认识到

remind sb. that... 使某人想起……

【句型】

Have you read *Little Women* yet? 你读过《小妇人》吗?

*Treasure Island* is about a boy who goes out to sea and finds an island full of treasures.《金银岛》讲述的是一个男孩出海并发现了一个满是宝物的岛屿的故事。

It made Sarah think about her family and friends back in the US. 它让萨拉想起了她在美国的家人和朋友。

## ☞ 典例剖析

请以"My Favorite Star"为题,写一篇文章介绍你最喜欢的明星。这个明星可以是歌手、演员、作家等。

写作要点:

1. 介绍你最喜欢的明星的基本情况(姓名、外貌、年龄等);

2. 你喜欢他/她的原因;

3. 他/她已经取得的成就;

4. 要用到现在完成时。

要求:1. 内容包括所有写作要点;

2. 条理清晰,行文连贯,可适当发挥;

3. 词数不少于 80 个。

**第一步:读题审题**

审
- 体裁:说明文
- 主题:介绍明星
- 人称:第一人称;第三人称
- 时态:一般现在时;现在完成时

**第二步:写作提纲**

首先,介绍最喜欢的歌手;

然后,介绍其成长经历;

最后,说明喜欢该歌手的原因。

**第三步:分层写作**

基础层:仿写句子

be from 来自,出自

【例句】这首歌出自美国历史上最成功的音乐家,乡村音乐歌手加斯·布鲁克斯。

The song is from a country music singer called Garth Brooks, the most successful musician in American history.

【仿写】马里奥,一个来自法国的客人。Mario, a guest is from France.

introduce A to B 把 A 介绍给 B

【例句】他在聚会上把我介绍给一位希腊姑娘。

He introduced me to a Greek girl at the party.

【仿写】我已经把她的歌曲介绍给我的好朋友,他也喜欢这些歌曲。

I have introduced her songs to my good friend who also likes the songs.

full of energy 充满能量

【例句】年轻人精力充沛。Young people are full of energy.

【仿写】当我听他的歌曲时,我感到幸福和充满能量。

I feel happy and am full of energy the moment I listen to his songs.

提高层:扩写句子

【例句】I like his music very much.(扩写原因"因为是流行音乐但有其他各种音乐的组合")

→I like his music very much because it is pop music but it has a mix of other kinds of music, such as R&B, rap, and rock.

【练习】Many of his songs are about the world we live in.(扩写细节"例如《稻香》鼓励人们即使在生活困苦时也不可放弃")

→Many of his songs are about the world we live in, such as *Dao Xiang* which encourages people not to give up even when life is difficult.

发展层:连句成章

## My Favorite Star

My favorite singer is Jay Chou (Zhou Jielun). It took him a few years to become famous. While Jay wrote songs for other pop singers, he also learned recording and sound mixing. His first album was released in 2000, and since then, he has released many famous albums. His albums have enjoyed great success in many countries, and his songs are popular with listeners of all ages.

I like his music very much. It is pop music, but it has a mix of other kinds of music, such as R&B, rap, and rock. Many of his songs are about the world we live in. One of my favorite songs is *Dao Xiang*, which encourages people not to give up even when life is difficult.

I feel happy and full of energy when I listen to his songs. I have introduced Jay's songs to my best friend, and he enjoys the songs, too!

师生互动:修辞润色

## My Favorite Star

My favorite singer is Jay Chou (Zhou Jielun). It took him a few years to become famous. While Jay wrote songs for other pop singers, he also learned recording and sound mixing. It was in 2000 that his first album was released(用强调句来强调时间), and since then, he has released many famous albums. His albums have enjoyed great success in many countries, and his songs are popular with listeners of all ages.

I like his music very much. It is pop music, but it has a mix of other kinds of music, such as R&B, rap, and rock. Many of his songs are about the world we live in. One of my favorite songs is *Dao Xiang*, which encourages people not to give up even when life is difficult.

I feel happy and full of energy when listening to his songs(主句和从句的主语相同时,可以把从句中的主语省略,改写成"when+doing"). I have introduced Jay's songs to my best friend, and he enjoys the songs, too!

## Unit 9 Have you ever been to a museum?

### ☞ 话题分析

本单元的话题是"有趣的地方",要求学生谈论去一些有趣的地方旅行的经历。针对该话题,常见的考查角度有两个:一个是介绍某一地区的情况(如位置、人口、大小、历史、名胜、气候等),体裁以说明文为主,时态多用一般现在时;另一个是谈论自己过去到某地旅行的经历,体裁以记叙文为主,时态多用一般过去时和现在完成时。

### ☞ 素材积累

**【单词】**

spring 春　season 季节　environment 环境　temperature 温度　population 人口　visit 参观

**【短语】**

amusement park 游乐场

history museum 历史博物馆

hear of 听说

go for a ride 兜风

have problems (in) doing sth. 做某事有困难

On the one hand…on the other hand… 一方面……,另一方面……

all year around 全年

place of interest 名胜

have a great time 玩得高兴

be famous for…因……著名

【句型】

Have you ever been to…? 你去过……吗?

It lies in… 它位于……

It has an area of… 它的占地面积约……

You can get there easily by… 你乘坐……就会容易到达。

It's unbelievable that… 不可思议的是……

The population is…/It has a population of… 人口是……

If you visit my hometown Lanzhou, you'll… 如果你来我的家乡兰州,你将会……

It is really a good place to do sth. 真是一个做某事的好地方

The most interesting place is… 最有趣的地方是……

## ☞ 典例剖析

> 假设以"有趣的地方"为主题展开讨论,请你根据自己对家乡的了解,用英语写一篇文章,介绍你的家乡。
>
> 要点:
>
> 1. 引出要介绍的家乡;
> 2. 介绍地理位置、人口、天气、景点、美食等;
> 3. 给出可以游览著名景点并享用美食的行程。
>
> 要求:1. 内容应包括以上要点,可适当发挥;
>
> 2. 80 个词左右。

**第一步:读题审题**

审
- 体裁:说明文
- 主题:有趣的地方
- 人称:第一人称
- 时态:一般现在时;现在完成时;一般将来时

**第二步:写作提纲**

第一段(开头,引入要介绍的地方):Have you ever been to…(填入地点)?

I think it's really…(填感受的词)

第二段(过程,具体介绍位置、交通、特色等):It is located in/lies in…(地理位置). It is famous for…(特色)…(地方) is home to…(人物). Besides, you can taste…(小吃)

第三段(总结,发出旅游号召):If you visit…(地点), you will…(填入感受)

**第三步:分层写作**

基础层:仿写句子

if you…如果你……

【例句】如果你在白天去看狮子、老虎或狐狸,它们可能正在睡觉。

If you go to see lions, tigers or foxes during the daytime, they'll probably be asleep.

【仿写】如果你去西安,你将有机会品尝那里美味的面条和饺子。

If you go to Xi'an, you will have an opportunity to taste the delicious noodles and dumplings there.

one great thing about… 一件关于……的大事(喜事)

【例句】新加坡的一大优点是全年的温度几乎是一样的。

One great thing about Singapore is that the temperature is almost the same all year round.

【仿写】关于西安的一个很棒的事情是它的景色很美。

One great thing about Xi'an is that its scenery is so beautiful.

提高层:扩写句子

【例句】Singapore is also an excellent place to try new food. (扩写原因"因为有来自许多国家的美食")

→Singapore is also an excellent place to try new food because there is much delicious food from many countries.

【练习】One great thing about Singapore is that the temperature is almost the same all year round. (扩写原因"因为地处热带地区")

→One great thing about Singapore is that the temperature is almost the same all year round because it is located in the tropics.

发展层:连句成章

Have you ever been to Xi'an? It's a beautiful city. It lies in the center of Shaanxi Province and has an area of about 10 000 square kilometers. With a history of more than 3 100 years, there are many places of interest in Xi'an, such as the famous Terra-Cotta Warriors and the amazing Bell Tower. Xi'an has four different seasons. If you go to Xi'an, you will have a chance to try the delicious noodles and dumplings there. One great thing about Xi'an is that it has convenient transportation. You can get there easily by train, plane or even bicycle.

师生互动:修辞润色

Have you ever been to Xi'an? It's a beautiful city which/that(去掉后一句主语 it,将前后两句改写为定语从句) lies in the center of Shaanxi Province and has an area of about 10 000 square kilometers. With a history of more than 3 100 years, there are many places of interest in Xi'an, such as the famous Terra-Cotta Warriors and the amazing Bell Tower. Xi'an has four different seasons. If you go to Xi'an, you will have a chance to try the delicious noodles and dumplings there. One great thing about Xi'an is that it has convenient transportation. It's easy for you to get there by train, plane or even bicycle.(用 it 做形式主语、不定式做真正主语的句式改写原句)

## Unit 10 I've had this bike for three years.

### ☞ 话题分析

本单元的话题是"生活环境",要求学生能够谈论周围的所有物和物品。最能全面体现本单元话题及语言运用能力的作文就是"谈论自己拥有的物品",这也是单元测试和中考试题中经常出现的作文之一。

### ☞ 素材积累

**【单词】**

生活环境:locate/lie 位于 development 发展 comfortable 舒适的 provide

提供 improve 改进;提高 crowded 拥挤的 be polluted 被污染 convenient 便利的

【短语】

used to be 过去是;曾经是

be located in/lie in 坐落于

take place 发生

take on a new look 呈现新面貌

change a lot/great changes have taken place 变化很大

enjoy a comfortable life 享受舒适生活

What's worse 更糟糕的是……

with the help of... 在……的帮助下

live a...life 过着……的生活

as time goes on 随着时间的推移

## ☞ 典例剖析

假设你是英文周刊 *English Weekly* 的特约小记者,请你以"A New Town"为题,根据下方要点写一则简讯,介绍你的家乡。

要点:1. 近五年来变化巨大;

2. 过去有很多大型工厂;

3. 现在已迁走所有工厂,空气变得清新,没有污染问题,人们的生活水平提高;

4. 对未来有一些展望。

要求:1. 简讯须包含要点的所有内容,语句通顺、意思连贯;

2. 可用自己的2—3句话表达合理想象,做适当发挥;

3. 80个词左右。

**第一步:读题审题**

审{
- 体裁:说明文
- 主题:家乡变化
- 人称:第三人称
- 时态:一般现在时;一般过去时;现在完成时

**第二步:写作提纲**

第一段:引出主题。

第二段:今昔对比。It used to be...but now it...

第三段:表达对家乡未来的展望,并号召他人来家乡看看。

**第三步:分层写作**

基础层:仿写句子

used to be 过去是……

【例句】我的家乡不再是过去的样子。它已经呈现出新的面貌。

My hometown is not what it used to be. It has taken on a new look.

【仿写】我的家乡以前有很多工厂。

There used to be many factories in my hometown.

take place 发生

【例句】在过去的几年中,我的家乡变化很大。

Great changes have taken place in my hometown in the past few years.

【仿写】这起车祸是什么时候发生的?

When did the traffic accident take place?

提高层:扩写句子

【例句】Trees and grass can be seen everywhere on either side of the road. [扩写修饰语“茂密的(树)”“绿色的(草)”]

→Thick trees and green grass can be seen everywhere on either side of the road.

【练习】The living standard of people has greatly improved.(扩写原因,用介词 with 扩写“随着社会的发展”)

→With the development of the society, the living standard of people has greatly improved.

发展层:连句成章

## A New Town

In the past five years, great changes have taken place in my hometown. The roads used to be narrow and crowded. Besides, the houses were old and small.

What's worse, due to many big factories, the air wasn't fresh enough to breathe. Sometimes, there was terrible smell. The river was polluted badly and there was rubbish in it.

Nowadays, the roads are wider and cleaner than before. It is really convenient for people to go out. We can choose different kinds of transportation to go anywhere. There are more tall buildings in the city. Most of us live in big beautiful houses now. What's more, the air is fresher because all the big factories were moved. Also, the sky is blue and the cloud is white. My hometown looks like a big garden with green trees, grass and colorful flowers.

With the help of the government, all of us are living a happier and richer life. I am sure as time goes on, our life will become better and better!

师生互动:修辞润色

### A New Town

In the past five years, great changes have taken place in my hometown. The roads used to be narrow and crowded. Besides, the houses were old and small. What's worse, due to many big factories, the air wasn't fresh enough to breathe. Sometimes, there was terrible smell. It is worth mentioning that(改写为主语从句,起强调作用) the river was polluted badly and there was rubbish in it.

Nowadays, the roads are wider and cleaner than before. It is really convenient for people to go out. We can choose different kinds of transportation to go anywhere. There are more tall buildings in the city. Most of us live in big beautiful houses now. What's more, the air is fresher because all the big factories were moved. Also, not only is the sky blue but the cloud is white(not only 置于句首,句子采用部分倒装,倒装句比原句结构更能体现学生的写作水平和技能). My hometown looks like a big garden with green trees, grass and colorful flowers.

With the help of the government, all of us are living a happier and richer life. I am sure as time goes on, our life will become better and better!

# 第五节　九年级全册

经过七年级和八年级的探索与练习,学生能够很好地适应两种分层写作模式。为让学生能继续通过这两种模式提高写作技能,笔者将九年级的十四个单元分为两部分:第一部分为九年级前十个单元,这一部分使用情景设置模式;第二部分为九年级后四个单元,这一部分使用“仿写+扩写+连句成章+师生互动”模式。上述教学安排有利于进一步提高学生的写作素养,实现课程标准要求的相应目标。

## Unit 1　How can we become good learners?

### ☞ 话题分析

本单元的话题是“学会如何学习”,要求学生能够完成以下写作任务:

①介绍个人的学习情况和学习方法;②针对他人在学习中遇到的问题,提出建议并提供帮助;③对于常见的学习方法,例如小组学习等,表达自己的看法和建议。

这类习作的体裁以议论文最为常见,时态多使用一般现在时,人称通常采用第一人称及第二人称。这类文章在写作时通常按照逻辑顺序来讲述方法和技巧。

**基本框架:**

第一段(引出话题):Dear…(人名)I'm glad to give you some advice about how to learn English. Here are…(ways/some pieces of advice…)

第二段(提出建议):My advice is that…

第三段(表达希望):I hope…[Best wishes! Yours,…]

## ☞ 典例剖析

> 假设你是朱欣,你的35中朋友李阳想要提高他的英语水平并写信向你寻求帮助,现在请你给他写一封回信,就学好英语的方法给他提一些建议。
>
> 要求:1. 文中不得出现任何真实的人名、校名及其他相关信息;
>
> 2. 不少于70个词;
>
> 3. 至少写3条建议。

**写作点拨:**

话题:提出学习建议

时态:一般现在时

人称:第二人称

**句型荟萃:**

Why not/Why don't you…? 你为什么不……?

You'd better… 你最好……

You could try to improve your English by… 你可以试着通过……来提高你的英语水平。

It's a good idea to… ……是个好主意。

**分层写作:**

基础层:根据语境,用所给词或短语的正确形式填空,使句意通顺。

| communicate | increase | pronounce | listen to | speak |
|---|---|---|---|---|

Dear Li Yang,

I'm glad to give you some advice about how to learn English. Here is the advice.

First, you can listen to English songs often. You can also watch CGTN at least three times a week. These will help you to correct your pronunciation and improve your listening. Second, it's a good idea to read some English newspapers and magazines. If you do this, you will not only increase your knowledge but also learn more words. Third, you could join an English club. It will provide you with many chances to communicate with others in English, and you can also make some friends. It's good for your spoken English.

I hope my advice will help you improve your English.

Best wishes!

Yours,

Zhu Xin

提高层:根据括号内所给信息填空。

Dear Li Yang,

I'm glad to give you some advice about how to learn English. Here is the advice.

First, you can listen to English songs often. You can also watch CGTN at least three times a week (至少一周三次). These will help you to correct your pronunciation and improve your listening (提高你的听力水平). Second, it's a good idea to read some English newspapers and magazines. If you do this, you will not only increase your knowledge (增加你的知识) but also learn more words. Third, you could join an English club. It will provide you with many chances(为你提供许多机会) to communicate with others in English, and you can also make some friends (交一些朋友). It's good for your spoken English.

I hope my advice will help you improve your English.

Best wishes!

Yours,

Zhu Xin

发展层:请把作文补全(九年级 Unit 1—10 发展层作文中的斜体部分为修辞润色)。

Dear Li Yang,

I'm glad to give you some advice about how to learn English. Here is the advice.

First, you can listen to English songs often, and you can also watch CGTN at least three times a week, *both of which* will help you to correct your pronunciation and improve your listening. Second, it's a good idea to read some English newspapers and magazines. If you do this, *not only will you* increase your knowledge but also learn more words. Third, you could join an English club, because it will *provide many chances for you* to communicate with others in English, and you can also make some friends. *There is no doubt that* it's good for your spoken English.

I hope my advice will help you improve your English.

Best wishes!

Yours,

Zhu Xin

## Unit 2 I think that mooncakes are delicious!

### ☞ 话题分析

本单元的话题是"节日",针对该话题,考试中常考的角度是介绍中国的传统节日,包括节日的名称、时间、含义及相关的活动等,有时还需要学生谈谈喜欢的节日及理由。体裁以说明文最为常见,时态多使用一般现在时,谈论个人喜好时通常用第一人称。这类文章在写作时通常按照时间顺序来介绍节日的起源及发展。

**基本框架:**

第一段(介绍节日):I'm very glad to tell you something about…, …is a traditional Chinese festival with a long history… is my favorite Chinese festival. It is celebrated in/on…

第二段(活动安排及感受):During this festival, people… It's my favorite festival because… It makes me feel… I think that….

第三段(结尾句):I hope that you can come to China next year and spend the festival with me.

## ☞ 典例剖析

最近,某英文报刊正在举办征文活动,主题是"弘扬中华传统文化,畅谈中国传统佳节"。请你以"My Favorite Chinese Festival"为题,写一篇英语作文,为本次活动投稿。

内容提示:

①简单介绍你最喜欢的中国传统节日的名称及时间等;

②讲述该节日的主要庆祝方式,比如人们的吃食及举办的活动;

③说明你对这个节日的感受及喜爱它的原因。

写作要求:

1. 内容包含以上要点;

2. 语言表达准确,语意通顺、连贯,70—80个词;

3. 书写工整、规范,文中不得出现真实姓名、校名和地名。

**写作点拨:**

话题:介绍节日

时态:一般现在时

人称:第一人称

**句型荟萃:**

I know that… is really fun. 我知道……是真有趣。

I wonder if they'll have… again next year. 我想知道他们明年是否会有……

I wonder whether… is a good time to visit… 我想知道……是否是个浏览……的好时候。

My favorite Chinese festival is… because… 我最喜欢的中国节日是……,因为……

**分层写作:**

基础层:根据语境,用所给词或短语的正确形式填空,使句意通顺。

| dumpling hope well get together important |
|---|

My Favorite Chinese Festival

It's known that there are many traditional festivals in China. Among them, I like the Spring Festival best.

It comes in January or February. It is a time for family members to get together. On the eve of the Spring Festival, all family members enjoy different kinds of food, such as dumplings and fish. We also watch the Spring Festival Gala and stay up late, hoping to have a new start in the following year.

The Spring Festival can not only make us feel love and happiness, but also the importance of home and family.

提高层:根据括号内所给信息填空。

## My Favorite Chinese Festival

It's known that there are many traditional festivals in China. Among them, I like the Spring Festival best/my favorite festival is the Spring Festival(我最喜欢春节).

It comes in January or February. It is a time for family members to get together(它是家庭成员团聚的时刻). On the eve of the Spring Festival, all family members enjoy different kinds of food, such as dumplings and fish(例如水饺和鱼). We also watch the Spring Festival Gala and stay up late, hoping to have a new start(希望有个新的开始) in the following year.

The Spring Festival can not only make us feel love and happiness, but also the importance of home and family(不仅能让我们感受到爱和幸福,而且也能让我们感受到家和家人的重要性).

发展层:请把作文补全。

## My Favorite Chinese Festival

It's known that there are many traditional festivals in China. Among them, I like the Spring Festival best.

It comes in January or February. *There is no doubt that* it is a time for family members to get together. *It's on the eve of the Spring Festival that* all family members enjoy different kinds of food, such as dumplings and fish. We also watch the Spring Festival Gala and stay up late, hoping to have a new start in the following year.

*Not only can the Spring Festival make us feel love and happiness but also the importance of home and family. Only by experiencing for yourself will you feel the happiness of Chinese people spending the Spring Festival.*

## Unit 3 Could you please tell me where the restrooms are?

### ☞ 话题分析

本单元的话题是"旅游"。学生需要学习介绍旅游线路以及礼貌地寻求帮助的句型。写作时,人称主要用第二人称,时态应用一般现在时,表示祝愿及希望时可用一般将来时或祈使句。

**基本框架:**

第一段(自我介绍):My name is…and I'm from…; I'll be coming to your…(place) on…for…

第二段(礼貌询问相关信息):When and where to stay/eat; necessary information about activities or transport.

第三段(感谢帮助你的人):I'm looking forward to your reply/I hope to hear from you soon/Thank you for early answer/Wish you good health and success in your work.

### ☞ 典例剖析

学者 Mrs. Marley 应邀将在本周五下午来你们学校做报告。假如你是九年五班魏明,请你根据以下提示用英语给 Mrs. Marley 写一封约 80 个词的电子邮件,告诉她如何到你们的学校。

提示:1. 在火车站乘坐 10 路公共汽车到渭源路南口下车,路程约 3 公里;然后沿着渭源路直走;

2. 在渭源路十字路口向左拐,会看到在右边有一个小区,小区门口有学校牌子;

3. 进入小区走大约 50 米后左拐,可以看到学校大门。

要求:根据提示内容进行写作,情节可适当发挥。

**写作点拨：**

时态：一般现在时

人称：第二人称

体裁：记叙文

**分层写作：**

基础层：根据语境，用所给词或短语的正确形式填空，使句意通顺。

| hang | get off | get to | accept | turn left | see |
|---|---|---|---|---|---|

Dear Mrs. Marley,

My name is Wei Ming from Class 5 Grade 9. I'm glad to hear that you have accepted our invitation to give us a speech. Now, let me tell you how to get to our school. First, take the No. 10 bus at the railway station and get off at the south entrance to Weiyuan Road. It's about three kilometers. Then go straight along the road.

When you come to the crossing of Weiyuan Road, turn left and you will see a community on your right. There is a school brand hanging at the gate of the community.

After entering the community about fifty meters, turn left and you will see the school gate. I will wait for you there at 2:30 p. m.

We are looking forward to seeing you.

Yours faithfully,

Wei Ming

提高层：根据括号内所给信息填空。

Dear Mrs. Marley,

My name is Wei Ming from Class 5 Grade 9. I'm glad to hear that you have accepted our invitation to give us a speech（听说你已经接受给我们做报告的邀请）. Now, let me tell you how to get to our school. First, take the No. 10 bus at the railway station（在火车站坐 10 路公交车）and get off at the south entrance to Weiyuan Road. It's about three kilometers. Then go straight along the road（沿这条路直走）.

When you come to the crossing of Wei yuan Road, turn left and you will see a community on your right. There is a school brand hanging at the gate of the community (有一块学校牌子挂在小区门口).

After entering the community about fifty meters, turn left and you will see the school gate (向左转,你就会看到学校大门). I will wait for you there at 2:30 p. m.

We are looking forward to seeing you.

Yours faithfully,

Wei Ming

发展层:请把作文补全。

Dear Mrs. Marley,

My name is Wei Ming from Class 5 Grade 9.

*To my joy*, *I heard the news that* you have accepted our invitation to give us a speech. Now, let me tell you how to get to our school. *What you first can do is to* take the No. 10 bus at the railway station and get off at the south entrance to Weiyuan Road. It's about three kilometers. *Next* go straight along the road.

*It's on the crossing of Weiyuan Road that you should turn left*, *at this time*, you will see a community on your right. There is a school brand *which hangs* at the gate of the community.

After entering the community about fifty meters, turn left and you will see the school gate. I will wait for you there at 2:30 p. m.

We are looking forward to seeing you.

Yours faithfully,

Wei Ming

## Unit 4 I used to be afraid of the dark.

### ☞ 话题分析

本单元的话题是"谈论生活变化"。该话题是中考常见话题之一,它贴近学生生活,容易引起学生的共鸣。在谈论生活变化时,描述过去的生活可以使用一般过去时或 used to do sth. 这一短语,描述现在的生活要用一般现在时。写作时要注意使用合适的时态。该类写作通常采用三段模式:第一段简单指出自己在生活中的变化;第二段介绍自己最主要和最大的变化;最后一段表达自己的愿望。学生要特别注意使用 used to do sth. 来描述过去的情况。

**基本框架:**

第一段(引起下文):My life has changed a lot in the last few years.

第二段(描述变化):I used to be…, but I'm not anymore now./I used to be…, but now I become much better in…

第三段(表达愿望和打算):I hope I will…/I will study much harder…

## ☞ 典例剖析

假如你是中学生李华,你校要举办个人成长写作大赛,题目是“How I've Changed!”。请你写一篇 80 个词左右的英语短文,介绍你在性格、外貌和爱好三个方面的变化,然后详述其中一个最重要的变化、变化过程以及原因。

注意:书写规范,要点齐全。

**写作点拨:**

体裁:说明文

时态:一般现在时;一般过去时(可用 used to do)

人称:第一人称;第二人称

**分层写作:**

基础层:根据语境,用所给词或短语的正确形式填空,使句意通顺。

| | | | | | |
|---|---|---|---|---|---|
| important | say | that | interest | read | |
| be | outgoing | knowledge | tall | change | |

How I've Changed!

I'm Li Hua, a middle-school student. I'd like to tell my changes in life. My life has changed a lot in the last few years. I used to be short, but now I'm one of the tallest students in my class. I used to be shy and quiet, but now I'm outgoing and I like to make friends. I used to hate reading, but now I have fallen in love with it.

The most important change in my life was becoming interested in reading. Last summer my best friend gave me an interesting book to read. I enjoyed it so much that I started to read other books. It was the most important change because reading gives me a lot of knowledge and makes me very happy. As a famous saying goes, "Reading makes a full man".

I hope I will be better and better.

提高层:根据括号内所给信息填空。

### How I've Changed!

I'm Li Hua, a middle-school student. I'd like to tell my changes in life. My life has changed a lot in the last few years(最近几年,我的生活已经发生了很大变化). I used to be short, but now I'm one of the tallest students in my class. I used to be shy and quiet(我过去腼腆文静), but now I'm outgoing and I like to make friends. I used to hate reading, but now I have fallen in love with it(我已爱上了它).

The most important change in my life was becoming interested in reading. Last summer my best friend gave me an interesting book to read. I enjoyed it so much that I started to read other books(我如此喜欢它以至于我开始看别的书). It was the most important change because reading gives me a lot of knowledge and makes me very happy(因为阅读给我很多知识并且让我非常快乐). As a famous saying goes, "Reading makes a full man".

I hope I will be better and better.

发展层:请把作文补全。

### How I've Changed!

I'm Li Hua, a middle-school student. I'd like to tell my changes in life. *It is in the last few years that my life has changed a lot. I used to be short, shy and quiet. I used to hate reading, too. But now I'm outgoing and one of the tallest students in my class, so I like to make friends. What's more, I have fallen in love with reading.*

*What's the most important change in my life? There is no doubt that I* was becoming interested in reading. Last summer my best friend gave me an interesting book to read. *So much did I enjoy it* that I started to read other books. It was the most important change because reading gives me a lot of knowledge and makes me very happy. As a famous saying goes, "Reading makes a full man".

I hope I will be better and better.

## Unit 5 What are the shirts made of?

### ☞ 话题分析

本单元的话题是"介绍某产品或物件",常见的写作任务是根据文字提示或生活实际,介绍某一产品或一些手工艺品等的产地或发源地,以及其制作材料、生产过程、用途、包含的特殊文化意义等。写作时要注意以下几个方面:

1. 能正确使用 be made of/from/in/by、be used for 等句型描述产品的信息;
2. 能在文章中正确使用主动语态和被动语态;
3. 能正确地描述产品的文化背景。

**基本框架:**

第一段(开门见山,直接表述需要介绍的对象):……(物品名称) is popular in my city/country...

第二段(描述物品的产地、原料、外观、制作方式、用途等):

(产地) It is made in...

(原料) It is made from/of...

(外观) There are different kinds of pictures on it, such as...

(制作方式) It is made by...

(用途) It is used for...

第三段(感受):It is good for... We would+祝愿

## ☞ 典例剖析

假如你叫李华，来自甘肃省天水市。近日，你的法国笔友 Alfred 发来一封电子邮件，他说要来天水旅游，询问你天水以什么而闻名，并让你推荐值得赠送朋友的纪念品。请你根据下面的要点提示给他回复邮件。

要点提示：

1. 以雕漆(carved lacquerware)闻名(有 2 000 多年的历史)，具有特殊意义；

2. 原材料：珍贵的纯天然材料，如桃红松(rosewood pine)、椴木(basswood)等木材，使用当地小陇山盛产的优质天然漆(lacquer)为原料；

3. 用途：可供人们观赏，同时也有一定的实用性；

4. 最佳推荐：茶盘(tea tray)。

**写作点拨：**

体裁：说明文

时态：一般现在时

人称：第三人称

**写作思路：**

第一段(引出介绍的产品)：My city, Tianshui in Gansu Province, is known for its carved lacquerware.

第二段（介绍产品，包括意义、原材料、用途、最佳推荐等）：

（意义）Carved lacquerware is special. It is treasure of traditional Chinese craftsmanship（中国传统工艺瑰宝），which has a history of over 2 000 years.

（原材料）It is made from precious pure natural materials, such as…

（用途）Carved lacquerware is used for life tools.

（最佳推荐）Every day many different kinds of carved lacquerwares are produced in Tianshui City. Tea tray is the most famous one. You can buy some for your friends and relatives.

第三段（邀请及祝愿）：Welcome to Tianshui City! I hope you will have a good time here!

**分层写作：**

基础层：根据语境，用所给词或短语的正确形式填空，使句意通顺。

| enjoy | produce | know | material | tradition |
|---|---|---|---|---|

Dear Alfred,

My name is Li Hua from Tianshui City of Gansu Province. Tianshui City is known for its carved lacquerware. Its carved lacquerware has been around for over 2 000 years. It is a treasure of traditional Chinese craftsmanship.

It is made from precious pure natural materials, such as rosewood pine, basswood and excellent quality lacquer from Mount Xiaolong. It is worth mentioning that carved lacquerwares are made to be enjoyed and used for life tools. Every day many different kinds of carved lacquerwares are produced in Tianshui, but the most famous one is the tea tray. It is not only beautiful but also practical. You can buy some for your friends and relatives.

Welcome to Tianshui City. I hope you will have a great time here.

Yours,

Li Hua

提高层：根据括号内所给信息填空。

Dear Alfred,

My name is Li Hua from Tianshui City of Gansu Province. Tianshui City is known for（因……而著名）its carved lacquerware. Its carved lacquerware has been around for over 2 000 years. It is a treasure of traditional Chinese craftsmanship.

It is made from（由……制成）precious pure natural materials, such as rosewood pine, basswood and excellent quality lacquer from Mount Xiaolong. It is worth mentioning that carved lacquerwares are made to be enjoyed［被制作的目的是用来观赏(用 make 的被动)］and used for life tools. Every day many different kinds of（许多不同种类的）carved lacquerwares are produced in Tianshui, but the most famous one is the tea tray. It is not only beautiful but also practical. You can buy some for your friends and relatives.

Welcome to Tianshui City. I hope you will have a great time here.

Yours,

Li Hua

发展层:请把作文补全。

Dear Alfred,

My name is Li Hua from Tianshui City of Gansu Province. Tianshui City is known for its carved lacquerware. Its carved lacquerware has been around for over 2 000 years. It is a treasure of traditional Chinese craftsmanship.

*What I'd feel like saying that carved lacquerware* is made from precious pure natural materials, such as rosewood pine, basswood and excellent quality lacquer from Mount Xiaolong. *There is no doubt that* carved lacquerwares are made to be enjoyed and used for life tools. Every day many different kinds of carved lacquerwares are produced in Tianshui, but *the tea tray is the most famous one*. It is not only beautiful but also practical. *Therefore*, you can buy some for your friends and relatives.

Welcome to Tianshui City. I hope you will have a great time here.

Yours,

Li Hua

## Unit 6 When was it invented?

### ☞ 话题分析

本单元的话题是"介绍小发明",要求学生用英文介绍一项自己的小发明。这类作文一般采用三段模式,体裁为说明文,时态通常用一般现在时,多用被动语态。

**基本框架:**

开头:主题句

正文:支持句,包括名字、时间、用途、指导和价格

结尾:结尾句(做推荐)

### ☞ 典例剖析

假如你的朋友刘莉发明的 A Special Pen 在科技大赛中获奖,被推选(choose)参加国际青少年科技创新大赛。请你用英语介绍一下该发明。

内容要点:

1. 笔有三种色,红、蓝、黑;能快速记录老师在课堂上讲解的知识。

2. 笔里装芯片,可以储存大量信息。

3. 笔可以拍照、录音,按一下笔的红色按钮,可以将记录的内容快速转换成文字,便于学习。

4. 笔可以发光,晚上可以做电灯使用。

注意:80 个词左右,书写规范。

参考表达:

芯片 microchip　分配 assign　发光 shine　转换 convert

青少年科技创新大赛 teenagers' science and technology innovation contest

**写作点拨:**

体裁:说明文

时态:一般现在时

人称:第三人称

**句型荟萃:**

I think… is a very useful invention. 我认为……是一项很有用的发明。

… was invented by… ……是由……(某人)发明的

… was invented in… ……是在……(某时间)发明的

**写作思路:**

第一段(简单介绍该钢笔的发明者及钢笔的用途):…was invented by… It is used for…, …is useful.

第二段(具体介绍该钢笔的用途):…comes with…program the words…write short form…

第三段(总结全文):contain up to… make changes…

**分层写作:**

基础层:根据语境,用所给词或短语的正确形式填空,使句意通顺。

| | | | | | |
|---|---|---|---|---|---|
| use | number | write down | word | take | make |

Liu Li is my friend. One of her great inventions got a prize in the science and technology competition and was chosen to attend the international teenagers' science and technology innovation contest. This invention is her special pen.

This special pen that is made of plastic has three colors which is red, blue and black and is used for taking notes of what teachers taught in class quickly. It is very useful for you to have a lot to write down. The pen comes with a microchip that can store a great number of information that you need. You can take photos and record with it; it can convert the information that you store into actual words so that you can study if you press the red button on the pen. Besides, the pen can shine to be used for night without light or electricity.

I think this special pen is a very useful invention. If you are a businessman, you can investigate and invest it.

提高层:根据括号内所给信息填空。

Liu Li is my friend. One of her great inventions got a prize in the science and technology competition and was chosen to attend the international teenagers' science and technology innovation contest. This invention is her special pen.

This special pen that is made of plastic（由塑料做成的）has three colors which is red, blue and black and is used for taking notes of（被用来记录）what teachers taught in class quickly. It is very useful for you to have a lot to write down（你有好多要写的东西时它是很有用的）. The pen comes with a microchip that can store a great number of information（可以储存大量的信息）that you need. You can take photos and record with it; it can convert the information that you store into actual words so that you can study（以便你能够学习）if you press the red button on the pen. Besides, the pen can shine to be used for night without light or electricity.

I think this special pen is a very useful invention. If you are a businessman, you can investigate and invest it.

发展层：请把作文补全。

Liu Li is my friend. One of her great inventions got a prize in the science and technology competition and was chosen to attend the international teenagers' science and technology innovation contest. This invention is her special pen.

*This special pen*, *made of plastic*, has three colors which is red, blue and black and is used for taking notes of what teachers taught in class quickly. It is very useful for you to have a lot to write down. The pen comes with a microchip that can store a great number of information that you need. *It's certain that* you can take photos and record with it; it can convert the information that you store into actual words so that you can study if you press the red button on the pen. Besides, the pen can shine to be used for night without light or electricity.

I think this special pen is a very useful invention. If you are a businessman, you can investigate and invest it.

## Unit 7 Teenagers should be allowed to choose their own clothes.

### ☞ 话题分析

本单元的话题是“谈论规章制度(家规、校规等)”,要求学生能够用英语描述被允许做和不被允许做的事情,并能针对这些事情发表自己的看法。体裁多为议论文,人称多为第一人称,时态应用一般现在时。

**基本框架:**

第一段(开篇点题):...be worried too much about...; I am glad to tell you something about...

第二段(具体介绍规矩):We are asked to be... Besides,...should be... Also, it's necessary to... We are not allowed to...; ...mustn't be... Only...are we allowed to...

第三段(表达期望):Hope this helps... Tell me if there's anything else you want to know.

### ☞ 典例剖析

> 众所周知,每个家庭都有自己的家规,你家也不例外。你不同意你家家规中的哪一条?为什么不同意?你认为这条家规应该如何修改?请你就这些问题写一篇日记来表达你的想法。

**写作点拨:**

体裁:记叙文

时态:一般现在时

人称:第一人称

**写作思路:**

第一段(亮明观点):One of the rules in my family is that... It's thought that..., but I don't agree with them.

第二段(讲述观点):First... Second... For these reasons, I think we children should be allowed to do…

第三段(表达愿望):I would like to do… I hope my family will understand me…

**句型荟萃:**

Each coin has two sides. 凡事皆有两面性。

A nation has its rule and a family also has one. 国有国法,家有家规。

**分层写作:**

基础层:根据语境,用所给词或短语的正确形式填空,使句意通顺。

| besides | strong | mean | fair | human |
|---|---|---|---|---|

Friday, July 19th

Every family has its own rules, and mine is no exception. Our family rules, which we refer to as "family values", have been passed down from generation to generation and have shaped who we are. With time going on, I couldn't agree more with the saying "Home is where the heart is".

However, there's one thing in my family rules that I strongly disagree with: we're not allowed to watch TV or use electronic devices after dinner. To me, this rule seems to have been created in the Stone Age, when humans were too afraid of the night and had no idea how technology could improve their lives. In our modern era, this rule doesn't make any sense at all. I mean, if I don't have my own devices, how can I relax after a long day of studying? It's unfair to deprive me of the one thing that could actually help me relaxed. Besides, there's so much to see and do on TV that I can learn new things and improve my knowledge base. If we're going to keep this rule, I suggest that it be reformed to include some flexibility. Maybe we can watch a movie or use our devices for a limited time after dinner, but only if it doesn't conflict with our homework.

I know this rule is meant to promote family relationship and reduce screen time, but it's also important for me to have some fun and relax after a long day. I don't want to be a robot all the time. I hope to have some balance in my life.

提高层:根据括号内所给信息填空。

Friday, July 19th

Every family has its own rules, and mine is no exception. Our family rules, which we refer to as "family values", have been passed down from generation to generation and have shaped who we are. With time going on, I couldn't agree more with the saying "Home is where the heart is".

However, there's one thing in my family rules that I strongly disagree with: we're not allowed to watch TV (我们不被允许看电视) or use electronic devices after dinner. To me, this rule seems to have been created in the Stone Age, when humans were too afraid of the night and had no idea how technology could improve their lives. In our modern era, this rule doesn't make any sense at all (这个规定根本没有任何意义). I mean, if I don't have my own devices, how can I relax after a long day of studying? It's unfair to deprive me of the one thing that could actually help me relaxed. Besides, there's so much to see and do (此外,有许多可看可做的事) on TV that I can learn new things and improve my knowledge base. If we're going to keep this rule, I suggest that it be reformed to include some flexibility (它应该被改革以增加一定的灵活性). Maybe we can watch a movie or use our devices for a limited time after dinner, but only if it doesn't conflict with our homework.

I know this rule is meant to promote family relationship and reduce screen time, but it's also important for me to have some fun (但对我来说玩得开心也是很重要的) and relax after a long day. I don't want to be a robot all the time. I hope to have some balance in my life.

发展层:请把作文补全。

Friday, July 19th

Every family has its own rules, and mine is no exception. Our family rules, which we refer to as "family values", have been passed down from generation to generation and have shaped who we are. With time going on, I couldn't agree more with the saying "Home is where the heart is".

However, there's one thing in my family rules that I strongly disagree with:

we're not allowed to watch TV or use electronic devices after dinner. To me, this rule seems to have been created in the Stone Age, when humans were too afraid of the night and had no idea how technology could improve their lives. In our modern era, this rule doesn't make any sense at all. I mean, if I don't have my own devices, how can I relax after a long day of studying? It's unfair to deprive me of the one thing that could actually help me *unwind*. Besides, there's so much to see and do on TV that I can learn new things and improve my knowledge base. If we're going to keep this rule, I suggest that it be reformed to include some flexibility. Maybe we can watch a movie or use our devices for a limited time after dinner, but only if it doesn't *interfere with* our homework *or family obligations*.

I know this rule is meant to promote family *bonding* and reduce screen time, but it's also important for me to have some fun and *unwind* after a long day. I don't want to be a robot all the time. I hope to have some balance in my life.

## Unit 8　It must belong to Carla.

### ☞ 话题分析

本单元的话题是"谈论神秘事物",相关的写作命题通常采用 Guided Writing 形式,要求学生根据中文或英文提示进行写作,或者根据图画内容发挥合理想象,描绘细节并将其连接成一个故事。学生需要能够正确使用 might、may、could、can、must、can't 等情态动词表述推测、分析及判断,并写出合理的理由。写作中要注意连词的使用。

**基本框架:**

第一段:引出主题。Background information about the mystery.

第二段:推断经过。How the mystery was solved.

第三段:推断结果。How the people in the neighborhood now feel.

## ☞ 典例剖析

假如你是九年级学生杜倩,你家所在的街区最近总能听到奇怪的声音,居民们对此有很多猜测:Victor Smith 认为是孩子们在玩耍时因为兴奋而发出的声音,Mrs. Smith 及其邻居们认为声音来自动物。大家最终知道了声音的真实来源:有不法分子砍伐树木,失去家园的浣熊因此每晚来垃圾箱找吃的。得知真相后,邻居们为浣熊感到难过,大家正在尝试帮助浣熊。请你以"No More Mystery in My Neighborhood"为题,写一篇 80 个词左右的短文,内容涵盖上述所有细节。

参考词汇:

不法分子 lawbreaker　居民 resident　浣熊 raccoon

护林站 ranger's station

**写作点拨:**

体裁:说明文

时态:一般过去时

人称:第三人称

**短语储备:**

blame on... 归咎于……

make space for...给……腾地方

lose one's home 失去家园

**分层写作:**

基础层:根据语境,用所给词或短语的正确形式填空,使句意通顺。

| mystery | live | neighbor | find | have fun |
|---|---|---|---|---|

### No More Mystery in My Neighborhood

These days, in my quiet neighborhood, something strange happened. Residents heard noises at night but no one knew why. Victor Smith thought that it was teenagers having fun while Mrs. Smith and their neighbors blamed it on animals.

We now know what was happening in the neighborhood. Some lawbreakers cut down trees in the nearby forest. This affected some animals living in the forest. A raccoon family lost their home and had problems finding food. The raccoons discovered food in my neighborhood's garbage bins, so they came back every night.

Now the mystery is solved. People in my neighborhood feel sorry for the raccoons and they are trying to help them.

提高层:根据括号内所给信息填空。

### No More Mystery in My Neighborhood

These days, in my quiet neighborhood, something strange happened. Residents heard noises at night but no one knew why. Victor Smith thought that it was teenagers having fun(它是孩子们在玩耍时因为兴奋而发出的声音) while Mrs. Smith and their neighbors blamed it on animals.

We now know what was happening(我们现在知道最近一直在发生的事) in the neighborhood. Some lawbreakers cut down trees in the nearby forest. This affected some animals living in the forest. A raccoon family lost their home and had problems/trouble/difficulty finding food(找吃的有困难). The raccoons discovered food in my neighborhood's garbage bins, so they came back every night.

Now the mystery is solved(谜底揭开了). People in my neighborhood feel sorry for the raccoons and they are trying to help them.

发展层:请把作文补全。

### No More Mystery in My Neighborhood

These days, in my quiet neighborhood, something strange happened. Residents heard noises at night but no one knew why. Victor Smith thought that it was teenagers *who had fun* while Mrs. Smith and their neighbors blamed it on animals.

We now know what was happening in the neighborhood. Some lawbreakers cut down trees in the nearby forest. This *had influence/effect/impact on* some animals *which lived in the forest*. A raccoon family lost their home and *the food was hard for them to find. The reason why the raccoons came back to my neighborhood's garbage bins every night is that they discovered food here.*

Now the mystery is solved. People in my neighborhood feel sorry for the raccoons and they are trying to help them.

## Unit 9 I like music that I can dance to.

### ☞ 话题分析

本单元的话题是"谈论个人及他人的喜好"。在生活中可供学生写作的话题有很多,如喜爱的音乐、舞蹈、电影、运动等。写这类作文首先要确定时态,多用一般现在时;其次要写清楚自己的喜好,并说明自己喜爱所提事物的理由,同时也可以谈谈自己的看法和感想。

**基本框架:**

第一段(引入话题):I love…and I often listen to music/watch movies/read…in my spare time.

第二段(喜欢的事物):I prefer music/drama/books that is/isn't/are/aren't …

第三段(表达愿望):I hope I can become a famous actor/writer…

### ☞ 典例剖析

假如你是李华,你的新加坡笔友 Lisa 来信说她对中国歌曲很感兴趣,想请你推荐你最喜欢的歌曲。《黄河兰州》是一首由歌唱家史宁广演唱的歌曲,得到了市民和网友的称赞,激励着兰州人民勇往直前。请你用英语写封回信,简要介绍你最喜欢的歌曲 *Yellow River · Lanzhou*,并谈谈你对这首歌曲的认识。

要求:1. 语言规范,语句通顺,可适当发挥;

2. 100 个词左右。

**写作点拨:**

体裁:应用文

时态:一般现在时;一般过去时

人称:第一人称;第三人称

**写作思路:**

第一段:My favorite… is…; the movie is about… I like/love/prefer/don't mind… that/which/who…

第二段:I like…because… It helps me… When I listen to/watch/read…, I feel… What's more…

第三段:In a word, the… is… It's well worth … because it teaches…

**分层写作:**

基础层:根据语境,用所给词或短语的正确形式填空,使句意通顺。

| play praise forge spare sing |
|---|

Dear Lisa,

I'm glad to hear from you. Now let me tell you something about my favorite song.

My favorite song is called *Yellow River · Lanzhou*. It is sung by Shi Ningguang. The song shows the great developing changes of Lanzhou in the recent years. In June, 2022, the song was published and got praised by the citizens and e-friends. From then on, the song inspired Lanzhou people to forge ahead. People of all ages fell in love with it and it became more and more popular. It has been played on many important occasions in Lanzhou. It was also sung in many schools of Lanzhou.

I like to listen to it in my spare time. It has a strong passion and high spirits. When I'm down or tired, it makes me excited. It is worth listening to. I hope that you will enjoy it too.

Best wishes!

Yours,

Li Hua

提高层:根据括号内所给信息填空。

Dear Lisa,

I'm glad to hear from you. Now let me tell you something about my favorite song.

My favorite song is called *Yellow River · Lanzhou*. It is sung by Shi Ningguang. The song shows the great developing changes of Lanzhou in the recent years. In June, 2022, the song was published and got praised by the citizens and e-friends(得到了市民和网友的称赞). From then on, the song inspired Lanzhou people to forge ahead. People of all ages fell in love with it(爱上了它) and it became more and more popular. It has been played on many important occasions(在许多重要场合已被播放) in Lanzhou. It was also sung in many schools of Lanzhou.

I like to listen to it in my spare time(在我空闲的时候). It has a strong passion and high spirits. When I'm down or tired, it makes me excited. It is worth listening to. I hope that you will enjoy it too.

Best wishes!

Yours,

Li Hua

发展层:请把作文补全。

Dear Lisa,

I'm glad to hear from you. Now let me tell you something about my favorite song.

My favorite song is called *Yellow River · Lanzhou*. It is sung by Shi Ningguang. The song shows the great developing changes of Lanzhou in the recent years. *It is in June of* 2022 *that* the song was published and got praised by the citizens and e-friends. From then on, the song inspired Lanzhou people to forge ahead. *Since people of all ages fell in love with it*, it became more and more popular. *What's more*, it has been played on many important occasions in Lanzhou. It was also sung in many schools of Lanzhou.

I like to listen to it *whenever I have spare time*. It has a strong passion and high spirits. *If I'm down or tired, I will listen to it because it makes me excited and better.* It is worth listening to. I hope that you will enjoy it too.

Best wishes!

Yours,

Li Hua

## Unit 10  You're supposed to shake hands.

### ☞ 话题分析

本单元的话题是"风俗习惯",介绍了一些国家的礼仪,如见面礼仪、餐桌礼仪等,谈论了在不同的场合应该做什么,能帮助学生了解不同国家的文化习俗。具体到书面表达中,本单元要求学生会写关于习俗(customs)、习惯(habits)和礼仪(manners)等方面的作文,并且要在作文中使用 be supposed to do 这一结构。

**基本框架:**

第一段(开头句):You must be excited about coming to China soon. Let me give you some suggestions and advice about Chinese customs.

第二段(正文):When you are doing sth. ..., you are supposed to.../you are expected to.../it's impolite to...

第三段(结尾句):Have a safe trip, and I look forward to meeting you soon!

### ☞ 典例剖析

假如你是朱华,你的法国笔友 Alice 要来兰州大学学习一段时间。她想了解一下兰州的风俗习惯。请你给她写封信,讲述兰州的一些习俗,以及如何表现才得体。

内容提示:

1. 可以从餐桌礼仪、家规、外出等方面做介绍;
2. 告诉她哪些应该做、哪些不应该做。

要求:1. 语句通顺,书写规范,可适当发挥;
　　2. 80 个词左右。

**写作点拨:**

时态:一般现在时

人称:第二人称

体裁:应用文

**分层写作：**

基础层：根据语境，用所给词或短语的正确形式填空，使句意通顺。

| shake hands | point at | make plans | expect | polite |
|---|---|---|---|---|

Dear Alice,

You must be excited about coming to Lanzhou University soon. Let me give you some suggestions about local customs.

When you are eating at the table in Lanzhou, it's <u>impolite</u> to stick your chopsticks into your food. You are not supposed <u>to point at</u> anyone with your chopsticks. You are not supposed to make noises while eating. In our house, you're supposed <u>to shake hands</u> with my father for the first time. You are not supposed to kiss when you meet my mother. You can say "nihao" to her with a big smile. When you go out with people, you <u>are expected</u> to call first. It's important <u>to make plans</u> to do something interesting or go somewhere together.

Have a safe trip, and I look forward to meeting you soon!

Best wishes,

Yours

Zhu Hua

提高层：根据括号内所给信息填空。

Dear Alice,

You must be excited about coming to Lanzhou University soon. Let me give you some suggestions about local customs.

When you are eating at the table in Lanzhou, <u>it's impolite to stick your chopsticks into your food</u>（把你的筷子插进食物里是没礼貌的）. You are not supposed <u>to point at anyone with your chopsticks</u>（用筷子指向任何人）. You are not supposed to make noises while eating. In our house, you're supposed <u>to shake hands with my father for the first time</u>（和我爸初次见面要握手）. You are not supposed to kiss when you meet my mother. You can say "nihao" to her with a big smile. When you go out with people, you <u>are expected/supposed to call first</u>（应该先打电话）. It's important <u>to make plans</u>（制订计划）to do something interesting or go somewhere together.

Have a safe trip, and I look forward to meeting you soon!

Best wishes,

Yours

Zhu Hua

发展层:请把作文补全。

Dear Alice,

You must be excited about coming to Lanzhou University soon. Let me give you some suggestions about local customs.

When you are eating at the table in Lanzhou, *it is worth mentioning that* it's impolite to stick your chopsticks into your food. *What's more*, you are not supposed to point at anyone with your chopsticks. *Besides*, you are not supposed to make noises while eating. *It's for the first time that* you're supposed to shake hands with my father in our house. You are not supposed to kiss when you meet my mother. You can say "nihao" to her with a big smile. When you go out with people, you are expected to call first. *You should do whatever you can* to make plans to do something interesting or go somewhere together.

Have a safe trip, and I look forward to meeting you soon!

Best wishes,

Yours

Zhu Hua

## Unit 11 Sad movies make me cry.

### ☞ 话题分析

本单元的话题是"情感与情绪",要求学生能根据文字提示或实际情况,简单描述某事物对人们的生活及情感所产生的影响。学生在写作时首先要把此事物介绍清楚,然后描述它对自己情感或情绪的影响,最后可以得出结论、总结经验或表达自己的观点。

## ☞ 素材积累

【单词】

happy 高兴　unhappy 不高兴　worried 担忧的　unforgettable 难以忘记的　willing 乐意的;愿意的

【短语】

argue with sb. 与某人吵架

cause an argument 引起争吵

refuse to do sth. 拒绝做某事

not…any more 不再……

a sense of relief 如释重负之感

lose face 丢脸

make mistakes 犯错;出错

be afraid of 害怕

【句型】

An experience was unforgettable. 一段经历难以忘记。

I argue with my friends. 我和我的朋友们吵架。

Li Hua and I were studying together. 我和李华正在一起学习。

Li Hua and I had different opinions about a math problem. 我和李华对一道数学题有不同的看法。

Li Hua and I didn't talk to each other. 我和李华互不说话。

I refused to admit it. 我拒绝承认它。

I didn't want to lose face. 我不想丢脸

This made me feel a sense of relief. 这使我有如释重负之感。

We shouldn't be afraid of making mistakes. 我们不该害怕犯错误。

## ☞ 典例剖析

明天英语课上的 Duty Report 该你发言了。请你以"An Unforgettable Experience"为题写一篇英语短文,给大家讲述你的一次因数学题观点不同而与好朋友李华争吵的难忘经历。

要求:1. 所给信息要在短文中体现出来;

2. 条理清楚,行文连贯,可适当发挥;

3. 文中不能出现真实的人名、地名等信息;

4. 词数不少于 80 个。

**第一步:读题审题**

审
- 体裁:记叙文
- 主题:难忘的事
- 人称:第一人称
- 时态:一般过去时

**第二步:写作提纲**

第一段(时间、地点、人物、事件):When did it happen? Where did it happen? Who…? What …?

第二段(感受和所获):How did it make you feel? Why? What did you learn from it?

**第三步:分层写作**

基础层:仿写句子

win/lose a competition 赢(输)比赛。

【例句】我们赢了这场足球赛。We won the football competition.

【仿写】由于我的失误,我们输掉了这场比赛。

We lost the competition because of my carelessness.

get into a fight with sb. 和某人起冲突

【例句】我昨天和我的搭档起冲突了。

I had got into a fight with my partner yesterday.

【仿写】上周,她和她的朋友在雁滩公园起冲突了。

Last week, she got into a fight with her friend in Yantan Park.

提高层:扩写句子

【例句】An experience is unforgettable.（扩写具体经历“我昨天和我最好的朋友李华吵架了”）

→An experience I think is unforgettable is that I argued with my best friend Li Hua yesterday.

【练习】I refused to admit it.（扩写原因“因为我不想丢脸”）

→I refused to admit it because I didn't want to lose face.

发展层:连句成章

### An Unforgettable Experience

An experience I think is unforgettable is that I argued with my best friend Li Hua.

On a Saturday in last term, Li Hua and I were studying together at his home. We had different opinions about a math problem. Such a little thing caused an argument between us. From then on, we didn't talk to each other. I knew that it was my fault, but I refused to admit it because I didn't want to lose face.

I didn't realize we wouldn't see each other anymore until I heard that Li Hua would move to another city with his parents. Two days before he left with his family, I said sorry to Li Hua. We made peace with each other. This made me feel a sense of relief.

No one is perfect. Everyone makes mistakes. We shouldn't be afraid of making mistakes. When we realize our mistakes, we should correct them at once.

师生互动:修辞润色

### An Unforgettable Experience

An experience I think is unforgettable is that I argued with my best friend Li Hua.

On a Saturday in last term, Li Hua and I were studying together at his home.

We had different opinions about a math problem. It is so little a thing that(改写为强调句型,并将 such a little thing 改写为 so little a thing) caused an argument between us. From then on, we didn't talk to each other. I knew that it was my fault, but I refused to admit it because I didn't want to lose face.

I didn't realize we wouldn't see each other anymore until I heard that Li Hua would move to another city with his parents. Two days before he left with his family, I said sorry to Li Hua. We made peace with each other, which (原句中的 this 使前后两句产生联系,此处用 which 将前后两句合并,构成非限制性定语从句) made me feel a sense of relief.

No one is perfect. Everyone makes mistakes. We shouldn't be afraid of making mistakes. When we realize our mistakes, we should correct them at once.

## Unit 12 Life is full of the unexpected.

### ☞ 话题分析

本单元的话题是"突发事件", 要求学生谈论过去发生的一些出乎意料的事情。针对该话题, 常见的考查角度是讲述自己过去的某次意想不到的经历, 或根据写作材料中提供的图片或文字描述等信息来讲述某人的经历。体裁以记叙文为主,时态以一般过去时和过去完成时为主,人称根据具体的题目要求来确定。写作中通常按照时间顺序行文。

### ☞ 素材积累

【单词】

luckily 幸运地 unluckily 不幸地 special 特别的;特殊的 unusual 不寻常的 suddenly 突然 unexpected 出乎意料的;始料不及的 till 到;直到 oversleep 睡过头;睡得太久

【短语】

by the time 到那时

without doing sth. 没/不做某事

help sb. with sth. 帮助某人做某事

on one's way to spl. 去某处的路上

too…to…太……而不能……

fall asleep 入睡

rush to 匆忙去做某事;迅速地去做某事

go off 爆炸;(电子设备)停止运转

show up 披露,揭露;露面

【句型】

When Mom called us, we had left for the countryside. 妈妈给我们打电话时,我们已经去了农村。

By the time she caught in touch with me, I had ridden my car to meet my father. 她和我联系上的时候,我已经开车去见我的父亲了。

Before English teacher came into the classroom, all the students had already begun to read aloud. 在英语老师进教室之前,所有的学生已经开始大声朗读了。

As I was watching TV, my mom was weaving her sweater. 当我在看电视时,我的母亲正在织毛衣。

What an unusual/a special/…day! 多么不同寻常/与众不同/……的一天啊!

## ☞ 典例剖析

同学们,在你初中的学习和生活中,一定经历过对你来说很特殊的日子(开心、感动、有趣、激动、难忘等)。请你用英语记录下这特殊的一天。

要点:

1. 对你来说,哪一天是一个特殊的日子;

2. 在这一天,发生了什么事;

3. 你的感受、收获,以及对你的影响。

要求:

1. 语句通顺,行文连贯;

2. 70 个词左右。

**第一步:读题审题**

审
- 体裁:记叙文
- 主题:记录特殊的一天
- 时态:一般过去时
- 人称:第一人称

**第二步:写作提纲**

第一段:I was too excited to fall asleep because the next day would be...(某个特殊的日子).

第二段:I rushed to ...(发生的具体事情)

第三段:What a special day! ...(感受、收获及影响)

**第三步:分层写作**

基础层:仿写句子

by the time 到那时

**【例句】**到他去世的时候,他已是一位百万富翁。

By the time he died, he was a millionaire.

**【仿写】**当我醒来的时候,时间已经是七点了。

By the time I woke up, it had been 7 o'clock.

help sb. with sth. 帮助某人做某事

**【例句】**我母亲经常帮助我学习物理。

My mom often helps me with my physics.

**【仿写】**我朋友来我家帮助我完成学校作业。

My friend came to my home to help me with my schoolwork.

提高层:扩写句子

**【例句】**I was too excited to sleep.(扩写原因"因为明天是我的生日")

→ I was too excited to sleep because the next day would be my birthday.

**【练习】**A bike knocked me down on my way to school.(扩写医生的建议)

→A bike knocked me down on my way to school and the doctor told me that I had to stay in bed for a few days.

发展层:连句成章

A Special Day

Once, I was too excited to fall asleep because the next day would be my birthday. The next morning, by the time I got up, it had already been seven o'clock. I rushed to school without eating breakfast.

Unluckily, a bike knocked me down on my way to school and the doctor told me that I had to stay in bed for a few days. I felt so sad. Luckily, my friends came to see me and helped me with my schoolwork. They also had a wonderful birthday party for me that evening.

What a special day!

师生互动:修辞润色

A Special Day

Once, I was so excited that I couldn't fall asleep(将 too excited to fall asleep 改为"so...that..."结果状语从句) because the next day would be my birthday. The next morning, by the time I got up, it had already been seven o'clock. I rushed to school without eating breakfast.

Unluckily, a bike knocked me down on my way to school and the doctor told me that I had to stay in bed for a few days. There is no doubt that (常见表达,使原句成为含有同位语从句的复合句) I felt so sad. Luckily, my friends came to see me and helped me with my schoolwork. They also had a wonderful birthday party for me that evening.

What a special day!

## Unit 13 We're trying to save the earth!

### ☞ 话题分析

本单元的话题是"保护环境",与此相关的写作任务通常要求学生根据文字提示、表格提示或实际情况，简单谈论各种环境问题及如何保护环境。写作时，要注意点明写作意图，阐释问题的重要性，找出解决问题的方法及发出号召。本话题常见的命题方式有提示性作文和看图作文等，体裁通常为议论文、记叙文。

### ☞ 素材积累

【单词】

environment 环境　protect 保护　save 拯救；节约　change 变化　pollution 污染

【短语】

give a speech on… 针对……做演讲

as for… 就……而言

be harmful to… 对……有害

save water 节约用水

set up 设立；建立；竖起；安装

play a part in… 在……中起作用

put sth. to good use 好好利用某物；充分利用某物

make a difference 有影响；起作用

shut off 关闭；切断

turn off the light 关灯

take action 采取行动

【句型】

It's my great honor to give a speech on sth. 我很荣幸就某事发表演讲。

The government has shut off many factories. 政府已关闭了许多工厂。

I remember to turn off the lights. 我记得要关灯。

I'll save water. 我会节约用水。

I always take my own bags to go shopping. 去购物时我总是自己带包。

It is time for us to take action to make a greener world. 我们是时候采取行动来创造一个更加环保的世界了。

Let's do something to make the world greener and greener. 让我们做些事情，使世界越来越环保。

## ☞ 典例剖析

假如你叫李梅,是第七十八中学(No. 78 Middle School)的一名学生。今年暑假,你将代表你校赴瑞士参加"模拟联合国"会议并做发言,此次会议的主题是"A Greener World"。你草拟了发言流程,请根据该流程写一篇英文发言稿。

流程:Introduce myself. (name, school, age...)

What China has done. (factories; new energy...)

How I go green. (lights, showers, bags...)

要求:1. 发言稿须根据所提供的流程自拟,要求语句通顺、意思连贯、符合题意;

2. 流程中的括号部分可供参考;

3. 90个词左右;

4. 发言稿中不得使用真实的个人及学校信息。

**第一步:读题审题**

审:
- 体裁:应用文
- 主题:环境保护
- 人称:第一人称;第三人称
- 时态:一般现在时;现在完成时

**第二步:写作提纲**

第一段:开篇点题。My name is... I am...years old. I'm studying at... It's my great honor to give a speech on...

第二段:环保措施。(政府措施)As for the Chinese government, it has... For example, it has shut off... Besides, it has...(我的措施)As a student, I can... Firstly, I always remember to... Secondly, I'll... Last but not least, I always...

第三段:发出号召。It's time for us to... Let's do something to make the world...

**第三步:分层写作**

基础层:仿写句子

take action 采取行动

【例句】我们应该采取行动以阻止我们的环境被污染。

We should take action to prevent our environment from being polluted.

【仿写】我们应该采取行动保护环境。

We should take action to protect our environment.

shut off 关闭

【例句】政府已经关闭了很多工厂。

The government has shut off many factories.

【仿写】我已经关闭了发动机(engine)。I've shut off the engine.

提高层:扩写句子

【例句】It has shut off many factories.(扩写定语从句"对环境有害的工厂")

→It has shut off many factories that are harmful to the environment.

【练习】I always remember to turn off the lights.(扩写时间状语"当我离开房间的时候")

→I always remember to turn off the lights when I leave the room.

发展层:连句成章

Good morning, everyone! My name is Li Mei. I am 15 years old. I'm studying in No. 78 Middle School. It's my great honor to give a speech on "A Greener World".

We all hope we will have a green world. As for the Chinese government, it has done many things to make it. For example, it has shut off many factories that are harmful to the environment. Besides, the government has studied new energy, such as the sun, wind and water.

As a student, I can also do a lot to make the world green. Firstly, I always remember to turn off the lights when I leave the room. Secondly, I'll save water when I take a shower. Last but not least, I always take my own bags to go shopping.

It is time for us to take action to make a greener world. Let's do something to make the world greener and greener.

师生互动:修辞润色

Good morning, everyone! My name is Li Mei. I am 15 years old. I'm studying in No. 78 Middle School. It's my great honor to give a speech on "A Greener World".

We all hope we will have a green world. As for the Chinese government, it has done many things to make it. For example, many factories that are harmful to the environment have been shut off by it (将原句改为被动句). Besides, the government has studied new energy, such as the sun, wind and water.

As a student, I can also do a lot to make the world green. Firstly, I always remember to turn off the lights when leaving the room(主句与从句的主语一致时,从句中的主语可省略,改为现在分词做状语的形式). Secondly, I'll save water when I take a shower. Last but not least, I always take my own bags to go shopping.

It is time for us to take action to make a greener world. Let's do something to make the world greener and greener.

## Unit 14 I remember meeting all of you in Grade 7.

### ☞ 话题分析

本单元的话题是"校园时光",需要学生回顾初中三年的学习生活并展望未来。学生应该能够叙述对自己有较大影响的某个人或某件事。写作时通常采用"三部曲",即:描写一次难忘的经历(包括人物、主要事件等);向对方提出建议;祝福对方,表达期待。人称常用第一人称和第三人称;写难忘的经历要用现在完成时或一般过去时,表达建议和祝福时可以用一般现在时或一般将来时。

### ☞ 素材积累

**【单词】**

person 人;个人 influence 影响;对……造成影响 encourage 鼓励 overcome 克服 thankful 感激;感谢 caring 乐于助人的;关心他人的;体贴人的 advice 建议

【短语】

take on new challenges 迎接新的挑战

have problems with sth. 某方面有问题、困难

day by day 一天天；逐日

the importance of… ……的重要性

help sb. with sth. 帮助某人做某事

【句型】

The person who has influenced me most is… 给我最深远影响的人是……

He encouraged/helped me to do better in… 他鼓励/帮助我在……做得更好。

When I face difficulty in my daily life, his spirit… 当我在日常生活中面对困难的时候，他的精神……

I am sure I will grow up better with… 我相信我会伴随着……成长得更好。

## ☞ 典例剖析

人生如旅，在你的成长过程中，许多人感动着你、影响着你，如父母、老师、朋友……最近你的家乡正在举行以“The Person Who Has Influenced Me Most”为题的中学生英语征文活动。女排自由人(libero)王梦洁深深地影响着你，请你根据下表中的内容要点写一篇征文以参加活动。

| | |
|---|---|
| 基本情况 | 1. 1995 年 11 月 14 日出生于山东济南，据说上小学时开始接触排球<br>2. 一直为梦想而奋斗<br>3. 2015 年入选中国国家女子排球队(中国女排) |
| 成功原因 | 1. 抓住机遇。<br>2. 自律。注重训练，保持了出色的身体状态和心理状态<br>…… |
| 对我的影响 | …… |

注意：100 个词左右。

**第一步:读题审题**

审
- 体裁:记叙文
- 主题:对“我”影响最大的人
- 人称:第一人称;第三人称
- 时态:一般过去时;现在完成时

**第二步:写作提纲**

第一段:引出话题。The person who has influenced me most is...(人名)

第二段:人物介绍。...(人名)was born in...(地点), in...(时间). In...(时间), he/she became an/a...(职业). What led...(人名) to success?

First... Second...

第三段:表达感激。...His/Her spirit keeps me going and encourages me to take on new challenges.

**第三步:分层写作**

*基础层:仿写句子*

never give up 决不放弃

【例句】面对困难决不放弃。Never give up when facing difficulties.

【仿写】我们决不放弃我们的梦想。We'll never give up our dreams.

influence sb./sth. 影响某人/某物

【例句】她的言行深深地影响了我。

What she did and said influenced me deeply.

【仿写】这个人深深地影响了我的生活。

This person influenced my life deeply.

*提高层:扩写句子*

【例句】The person is Wang Mengjie.(扩写定语,用定语从句表达“对我影响最大”)

→The person who has influenced me most is Wang Mengjie.

【练习】She didn't lose heart or give up.(扩写时间状语“即使是在她遇到一些困难的时候”)

→She didn't lose heart or give up even when she met some difficulties.

发展层:连句成章

The Person Who Has Influenced Me Most

The person who has influenced me most is Wang Mengjie, a female volleyball libero. She was born in Jinan, Shandong Province in November 14th, 1995. Now she is a highly skilled and experienced player who has made a significant contribution to the team's performance.

It's said that she started playing volleyball when she was in elementary school. As she was small, she had a big dream to play volleyball. Therefore, she was fighting for her dream all the time. As a saying goes, "Where there is a will, there is a way." In 2015, she was selected to the Chinese women's volleyball team.

What led Wang to success? First, it is the opportunities that made her successful. She tried her best to seize every opportunity she met. Secondly, self-discipline plays an important role in her success. She paid much attention to her training and maintained an excellent physical and mental state.

Wang Mengjie has influenced me a lot. Whenever I face any trouble in study, her spirit keeps me going on and encourages me to take up new challenges.

师生互动:修辞润色

The Person Who Has Influenced Me Most

The person who has influenced me most is Wang Mengjie, a female volleyball libero. She was born in Jinan, Shandong Province in November 14th, 1995. Now she is a highly skilled and experienced player who has made a significant contribution to the team's performance.

It's said that she started playing volleyball when she was in elementary school. Small as she was(运用部分倒装,使句子更为高级), she had a big dream to play volleyball. Therefore, she was fighting for her dream all the time. As a saying goes, "Where there is a will, there is a way." In 2015, she was selected to the Chinese women's volleyball team.

What led Wang to success? First, it is the opportunities that made her successful. She tried her best to seize every opportunity she met. Secondly, self-discipline plays an important role in her success. She paid much attention to her training, maintaining an excellent physical and mental state(现在分词做状语,表示与主句谓语同步进行).

Wang Mengjie has influenced me a lot. Whenever I face any trouble in study, her spirit keeps me going on and encourages me to take up new challenges.

# 参考文献

[1] 冯裕彦. 隐性分层教学对初中生英语阅读能力影响的研究[J]. 科教导刊(电子版),2022(14):251-252.

[2] 黄文剑. 隐性分层教学在初中英语课堂中的应用探讨[J]. 中学生英语,2018(22):79.

[3] 霍燕. "隐性分层教学法"在初中英语写作教学中的"分"与"不分"[J]. 甘肃教育研究,2021(3):50-54.

[4] 李军强. "隐性分学法"在初中英语写作教学中的应用研究[J]. 教育教学论坛,2021(35):161-164.

[5] 吕桂香,王彦林. 隐性分层教学在初中英语课堂中的应用探讨[J]. 科普童话,2019(23):36.

[6] 梅德明,王蔷. 义务教育英语课程标准(2022年版)解读[M]. 北京:北京师范大学出版社,2022.

[7] 唐从刚. 隐性分层教学在初中英语课堂教学中的应用[J]. 中学课程辅导(教师通讯),2017(2):25.

[8] 王笃勤. 英语教学策略论[M]. 北京:外语教学与研究出版社,2002.

[9] 徐伟. 隐性分层模式在初中英语教学中的应用研究[D]. 延边:延边大学,2016.

[10]杨会丽. 隐形分层教学在初中英语课堂中的应用探讨[J]. 校园英语,2018(32):182.

[11]中华人民共和国教育部. 义务教育英语课程标准(2022年版)[M]. 北京：北京师范大学出版社,2022.
[12]朱丽莉. 隐性分层教学在初中英语课堂中的应用[J]. 新智慧,2018(23):86.